30 Days to a More Spiritual Life

SHANA ABORN

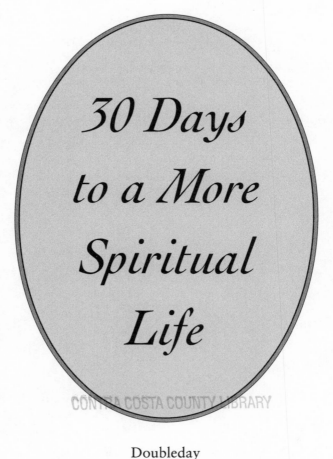

30 Days

to a More

Spiritual

Life

Doubleday

New York   London   Toronto   Sydney   Auckland

PUBLISHED BY DOUBLEDAY
a division of Random House, Inc.
1540 Broadway, New York, New York 10036

DOUBLEDAY and the portrayal of an anchor with a dolphin are trademarks
of Doubleday, a division of Random House, Inc.

This book, and certain chapters herein, are based on an article that
originally appeared in the November 1998 issue of *Ladies' Home Journal*.

Library of Congress Cataloging-in-Publication Data

Aborn, Shana.
30 days to a more spiritual life / Shana Aborn.—1st ed.
p.   cm.
1. Spiritual life.   I. Title: Thirty days to a more spiritual life.
II. Title.
BL624 .A26 2000
291.4'4—dc21
00-034582

ISBN 0-385-49785-7

To my family,
to John,
and to everyone
who believes

Acknowledgments

T<small>HIS</small> <small>BOOK</small> would not be here today if not for an article assignment from *Ladies' Home Journal*, the magazine I have been proud to call my employer for the last thirteen years. My thanks to editor-in-chief Myrna Blyth for generously allowing me to expand *30 Days* into book form, and to the entire editorial staff for supporting me along the way.

My thanks, also, to:

My agent, Noah Lukeman, for reading a 1,500-word article and seeing potential in it for something more.

Eric Major of Doubleday, for taking a chance on the "lovely jewel" (his words, not mine), and senior editor Trace Murphy, for making my entry into book writing so enjoyable and for being far kinder to my text than I would have been.

The experts I interviewed in the course of researching the original article and the book, who helped me realize that God is accessible in the simplest ways.

The volunteers from all over the country who tried the exercises in an effort to give their spiritual lives a boost, and who shared their own accounts of daily spirituality.

Rabbi Joel Goor of the Metropolitan Synagogue in New York, for helping me rediscover the joy of faith and the strength of religious community.

Natasha Jitomirskaia, Cathy Schwartzman and Dan Pincus, past and present cantors at Metropolitan, for showing me the importance of making a joyful noise when no other form of prayer will do.

The many amazing people who have made my life so rich—among them relatives, in-laws, grade-school friends, Tau Ep soulmates, fellow thespians, coworkers and fellow writers.

John O'Hare, my wonderful husband, partner and best friend, for his love, inspiration, humor, support and guidance (especially the guidance involving his leading me to the computer and reminding me of impending deadlines).

My parents, Murray and Barbara Aborn. In addition to giving me their love, encouragement and creative genes, they laid a solid foundation of faith and tradition for me—and gave me the freedom to embrace it for myself. And David, for being such a terrific, caring brother, and for providing me with a great opening anecdote.

And last but never least, to *Adonai Eloheinu*, for giving us life, sustaining us and enabling us all to reach this day.

Introduction

MY BROTHER became a bar mitzvah in a convent.

Okay, it wasn't exactly a convent, it was the library of a Catholic school. And this wasn't a weird new modern interfaith religion, either. It's just my way of explaining that my religious background was a little different from the norm.

Though my parents chose not to join a synagogue after they married and started their family, they still wanted their children to grow up respecting and knowing something of their Jewish heritage. As it happened, there was a nonsynagogue-affiliated organization in our area that offered High Holiday services and a children's Hebrew school. So every Sunday, my brother and I learned our *alefs* and *bets*, sang the Israeli national anthem and nibbled our Purim hamentaschen in church basements and schoolrooms or whatever space the board was renting that year.

My family celebrated Rosh Hashanah and Yom Kippur inside a Presbyterian church, the modern stained-glass Resurrection images beaming down on us as we held our little black Union Prayer Books and sang songs asking God to be merciful and forgive our sins. It didn't seem all that strange to me. The Sunday school teachers had taught us that God was everywhere, so I didn't feel as though my prayers were being ignored simply because I wasn't in the right house of worship.

But when my seventh-grade class separated into two groups—those who would receive intensive tutoring toward their bar and bat mitzvah ceremonies and those who would continue their basic education and graduate with a simple ceremony the following year—I demanded to stay in the group that offered the path of least resistance.

Why? Because at twelve, I was a major brat. Hormones, boredom and a wide rebellious streak were kicking in at full force, and now that I could see the light at the end of the tunnel of religious education, I saw no need to knock myself out learning an entire Torah passage when I had struggled mightily for seven years just to be able to read *abba ba* ("Father is coming"—the equivalent of "See Spot run") in Hebrew.

But there was a part of me that also recognized the hypocrisy of preparing for a coming-of-age passage meant to propel me into becoming an active member of a culture I had barely bothered to try to understand, much less love. To me, Judaism was a handful of small rituals: candles on Friday nights, costumes at Purim, a ten-minute lesson on freedom at Passover just before the Seder meal, the agony of starving on Yom Kippur and feeling awkwardly conspicuous every winter when ours was the only house in the neighborhood not blazing with colored bulbs and plastic Nativity figures.

My parents tried to instill a love of their heritage in me—the faith my father had been born into and the one my mother had proudly chosen when she converted at marriage. But somehow, I never felt a compelling sense of spirituality: being connected to a people, to a tradition or to a great and awesome Power at the center of the universe. I was too absorbed in keeping up my grades, reading Judy Blume novels and despairing of getting a date before the end of the decade to care much. I was a daughter, a sister, a friend, a student, a writer, an actress—but not a spiritual being. Why did I need God, anyway?

Still, there was something of Judaism that clung to me, like a piece of stubborn lint on a sweater. I went to a highly respected college in a Southern town not known for its vast Jewish population. This meant that not only did I know the heady thrill of being away from home for the first time, but I was also free to live a liberated, religion-free life. It should have been exciting; instead, it was isolating.

Being around so many non-Jewish students, many of whom had strong ties to their own churches, made me realize not only how different I was, but how much I missed being connected to the traditions I had grown up with. They may have been a little unorthodox, but they were traditions nonetheless. It wasn't long before I sought out the small Jewish student union, and almost immediately, I felt like less of an outsider.

But it didn't stop there. I couldn't bring myself to eat bread at Passover (not even the bagels offered by our well-meaning but uninformed cafeteria). I lit my menorah at Chanukah and taught my roommate how to say the Hebrew blessing. I skipped classes to attend High Holiday services in the college's little temple. I even fasted all the way to sunset on Yom Kippur—and believe me when I say that this was a big deal. I used to dread the thought of being hungry all day more than the idea of not being absolved of the past year's sins. I could have easily blown off five thousand years of tradition and sneaked out to Baskin-Robbins.

And yet there was something that felt so . . . right about it. Maybe it was the familiarity of continuing the tradition. Maybe it was the maturity of young adulthood that allowed me to realize that going without food for a day wasn't the end of the world. But most of all, celebrating the holiday made me feel a very comforting connection. I was connecting to my family, a few hundred miles away, doing the same thing. I was connecting to Jews all over the world, sitting in temples both magnificent and humble, intoning the same chants and in the process creating a larger song of humanity and community. I was connecting to Jews thousands of years ago, for whom the ritual was still new and evolving.

And, I realized, I was connecting to God. By taking

time out from my hectic school schedule and separating from the world for a few hours, I was focusing on something greater than myself. Without the comfort of a full stomach, I could reflect more easily on the discomforts I had caused to others and become more repentant of them. In the tiny sanctuary, there was a sense of awe that filled the room, and I was part of it. And because I had chosen to worship of my own free will, that made the day all the more important. I think my prayers were more heartfelt for it. (Okay, I admit that some of those prayers were pleas to make sunset come quickly so I could head to the caf before they ran out of Salisbury steak. A saint I'm not.)

I wish I could say that I graduated from college a more committed and observant Jew. But it didn't quite happen that way. Life went off into a gallop. I moved back home, landed my first journalism job and then got transferred to New York a year later. There, I met the nice Catholic man who would become my husband. With one thing and another, spirituality got crowded out again.

Still I held tight to the holiday traditions, which were even more of a comfort after I moved north. Even though I knew only a handful of people, somehow I always got invited to seders, and there was no problem finding a temple for the High Holidays.

Then, about five years ago, I came across a synagogue in midtown Manhattan that advertised itself as being open to all newcomers, as well as interfaith families. The temple shared space with a Unitarian church, so right away, the atmosphere felt familiar. I was drawn to their emphasis on music, and the sounds of the cantor, choir and organ swelling and rising toward the high brick ceiling seemed to fill my soul to overflowing. This was what it was like to worship with joy and song. All of a sudden, I felt the connectedness again.

It took me another two years to decide to attend an occasional Sabbath service there, but when I did, I discovered a wonderful sense of peace deep within. It was magical to be able to leave the hectic office and step into the calm of the temple. In just an hour's time, I could forget about the past week—and all I had to do was listen, learn and drink in the atmosphere of gratitude. After sharing wine and challah bread with the congregation, I would leave, feeling as refreshed as if I'd just stepped out of a hot bath.

The following year, the rabbi announced that he would be conducting Hebrew lessons for adults who wanted to brush up on their skills. By then, I was eager to learn enough about the language to be able to follow the prayers, and I was surprised to learn that it was easier than I'd remembered it being when I was ten.

When Rabbi Goor suggested that I study for my bat mitzvah, I knew the time was finally right. For once in my life, I wanted to step up and take my place among the congregation and to show my parents that I had chosen to follow the course they had set for me. More than that, though, I wanted to make even more of a commitment to my own soul and to its relationship to God.

It wasn't the elaborate ceremony you sometimes read about in the papers. I didn't have three hundred guests, and the reception afterward consisted of fruit and cookies in the temple social hall, not at the Waldorf-Astoria with a Renaissance theme and a four-tier cake. But it meant more to me than any birthday party I'd ever had. It could have taken place in a convent, an ashram, a hogan or under the stars on a mountaintop, and it would have been just as special.

Yet even before the big day, something was happening within me that seemed both unfamiliar and comfortable. I couldn't tell you exactly when it happened, but I started becoming more aware of everything—from the seasons to the taste of wine to the feel of a hot morning shower. It wasn't a "Wow! Look at this!" realization, but a gradual slide into awareness.

Going to temple had become such a part of my weekly routine that it didn't surprise me when I caught myself singing Hebrew songs while doing the dishes. More surprising was feeling the urge to pray even when I wasn't seated in a pew. Slowly, I went with the feeling, sending a few quick thoughts heavenward on the bus during my morning commute.

The peace I felt during worship felt so good that I looked for ways to replicate that sense of calm at other times. At the time, I was using my lunch hour to get some exercise by walking twenty or thirty blocks; it wasn't long before I realized that my daily strolls were a peaceful experience. Being around nature helped, too—I could lose myself in watching a spider spin a web, watching the late summer sky turn to pink and purple or checking out tree branches to see if I could catch the exact moment in which their buds unfurled into leaves.

I was finding my own sense of spirituality without even trying. And it felt wonderful.

I'm an editor and writer for *Ladies' Home Journal*. At the time I was studying for my ceremony, the magazine was running a series of articles on various ways to become healthier, less stressed and more informed in the course of thirty days (on the theory that it takes a month to establish a habit firmly). Since the subject of spirituality hadn't yet been covered, I suggested that we do it as part of the series. Luckily, my editors liked it and assigned the story to me. Using what I had already discovered for myself, with extremely helpful input from spiritual authors and clergy members, I put together a four-week plan—and learned a lot along the way.

When an agent who read the article called me to suggest that it had the potential to be a book, I realized he was right. The story covered some ground, but not nearly all of it—and what it did cover was restricted by space. More important, however, I realized that there might be readers out there who would be curious to learn still more about simple spirituality.

These days, it seems that more and more of us are looking for a satisfaction in our lives that goes beyond having a successful career, a comfortable lifestyle and access to the latest high-tech gadgets and conveniences. Increasingly, we're looking to the spiritual world for the answers we can't find anywhere else.

But most of us have never been touched by an angel and probably wouldn't realize it if one were poking us with a nail-studded two-by-four. Wearing crystals and carrying totems may be spiritually fulfilling for some people, but for others, these types of rituals may seem too unfamiliar to bring us closer to our concept of a Higher Power. It's hard enough finding the energy to clean the house on a semiregular basis, much less clean our chakras. And though we may put in an appearance at church or temple every so often, are we coming away feeling refreshed down to the soul, or just satisfied that we've done our duty for the week to rack up some heavenly brownie points in an unseen ledger?

That's where this book comes in. Incorporating concepts from the original *LHJ* article, plus additional insights and ideas, this guide is designed to help you find personal, comprehensible ways to tap into your spiritual side in every aspect of your daily life. Growing closer to God means not only communicating through prayer and meditation, but understanding and appreciating ourselves and our world, as well. It's discovering all the holy moments in the day that we often overlook—and creating some of our own. It's in the way we act toward others, conduct our business, even express our physical love.

This book is divided into four one-week sections, each emphasizing a different spiritual theme. Each section has a number of exercises, ranging from very basic ones that need little or no effort to more involved ones that may need more thought and commitment. Some are rituals that should be done every day for the full month; others can be done a few times a week; and others are long-term projects that you can begin now and continue long after the month is over.

It may be easiest to begin on the first of the month, but you can start your Week 1 whenever you like. You don't even have to start on a Sunday or Monday. If you'd rather launch your spiritual month on a Thursday, go for it; just remember to start the Week 2 exercises the following Thursday.

You can try as many or as few of the exercises as you like, but once you choose one, commit to doing it regularly until the month is over. Don't worry if they feel awkward or unusual at first. Habits take time to develop. You'll find that it becomes much easier with practice to pray, walk mindfully or develop a personal ritual. However, if you miss a day or a week, don't agonize over it, and don't say, "Well, I blew it—I might as well forget the whole thing." Just chalk it up to the process of learning and start fresh the next day. Part of being a spiritual person is learning to be gentle with yourself.

On the other hand, if there are any exercises that make you feel totally uncomfortable, don't force yourself to do them. This is supposed to be an enjoyable month. (You might want to ask yourself why you feel this way about that particular project, however. You might learn something interesting about yourself in the process.)

Don't expect miracles, either. You're not going to find ultimate enlightenment in just one meditation session or, for that matter, in a hundred. The point isn't to become perfect or more "religious"—it's to increase your awareness of yourself as a spiritual being and, I hope, to bring you closer to God as you perceive Him. You may not feel utterly transformed, but chances are you'll at least feel more peaceful, less stressed and eager to continue exploring your spiritual path.

That's what happened to me. I'm hardly a perfect person as a result of all this. (Just ask anyone who knows me. *Anyone.*) I'm nowhere near absolute divine enlightenment, and there are those who would even consider me a less than devout Jew. That's fine with me. It's much more fun to be imperfect and learn more about myself, my beliefs and God on a daily basis than to claim I know everything there is to know on the subject. That's why this book focuses on achieving a "more" spiritual life. There's always room for more.

A COUPLE of cautionary notes: In writing this, I put forth the assumption that there is a single force, energy, spirit or Higher Power in the universe that has at least some control over the world. For the sake of simplicity and because it's the term I'm personally most comfortable with, I refer to it as "God." If you prefer to call this force by another name, by all means, do.

The exercises also draw from a number of faiths and traditions; some of them will be familiar to you, others less so. If you're looking for a guidebook that will tell you exactly what to believe, or if you feel you may be offended by a spiritual book that doesn't operate by the precise principles you believe, to be true, then you'd probably be better off looking elsewhere for guidance. Though I obviously come from one particular background of faith, I've tried to keep an open mind here, and I hope you will do the same.

Let's start the journey.

Week 1

Discovering
Yourself

Spirituality, simply put, is who you are and how you are in relation to whatever force you believe guides your universe. This week, you'll focus on the "who," because knowing yourself is almost as much of a challenge as knowing God.

First, you'll determine exactly what your beliefs are, and then you'll learn to become more comfortable with yourself as a spiritual being. From there, you'll start the exhilarating process of communicating with God in a personal way. By the end of the week, you should be more aware of yourself, your actions and motivations, and more receptive to the idea of being with God on a daily basis.

Write Your Credo

BEFORE STARTING your quest for daily spirituality, it's important to know what spirituality means to you. And you can't do that if you don't know exactly who you are and what belief systems guide you in all circumstances.

Back in college, I minored in theater, and for several semesters I studied playwriting with an excellent professor. At the beginning of the year, he would give us an exercise that we had to complete before we even began to think about creating a plot for our first scripts. The assignment was to take some time alone to write our own personal credos, answering the question: "What do you believe?" We didn't have to share our essays with the class; they were meant to be a guide to help us write plays that expressed our deepest feelings.

Nothing to it, right? Ha. If you've never sat down and made yourself think seriously about your beliefs, you'll find that it's harder than it seems. Back in school, I struggled terribly with my credo, not daring to delve far enough into my innermost self to put my beliefs on paper. As a result, the one-acts I wrote that semester were glib, superficial and highly impersonal. I wasn't writing about topics I fiercely cared about. I didn't take a stand. I didn't believe what I wrote even as my fingers moved across the keyboard. Sure, I could come up with witty and literate lines, but I couldn't create believable characters facing crises audiences could identify with. So it is with spirituality. If you can't come to terms with your own beliefs, it'll be that much harder to be true to yourself, much less draw closer to the awe and mystery of God.

So your challenge now is to write your own credo. You may find it easiest to start with the basics: "I believe the Father, Son and Holy Spirit exist and reign over us from heaven." "I believe earth spontaneously arose from a cosmic explosion." "I believe that people are (or aren't) reincarnated after death." Then go on from there. Be as creative as you like; think of Kevin Costner's speech in *Bull Durham* that includes everything from his theory on Lee Harvey Oswald to AstroTurf to "long, slow, deep wet kisses that last for three days."

You can include negative statements—"I believe mankind is inherently cruel"—but avoid self-deprecating ones: "I believe I'm too fat" or "I believe I need a better job." The object isn't to subject yourself to harsh scrutiny, but to find out where your heart and soul truly lie so that you can use the information to discover your own spirituality.

Most importantly, be honest. Don't say that you believe something just because you think you "should," because you heard it every week in church or because you know that your husband or mother or best friend believes it, so therefore it must be right, right? No one's going to grade or judge your credo, so the only person you'll be lying to is yourself. If you write a statement that doesn't feel exactly right, explore it for a while. Why do you think it's part of your belief system? Would you feel comfortable defending your view against someone with a different opinion? You might be surprised at what you discover.

Once you've said all you feel you want to say, put your credo away for the moment. We'll return to it later.

Living Mindfully 101

IF YOU'VE READ other books on spirituality, you've probably seen the concept of "mindfulness" come up. It's considered crucial to live a mindful life and make the most of each moment by being aware of every action. But when you're rushing from task to task, looking ahead to what you have to accomplish in the next minute, hour or day, it's tough to keep your mind on any one thing, much less be aware of what you're doing.

How many times during the course of your normal day do you do one or more things at once? Do you watch the morning shows while you eat breakfast? How about reading while you ride the bus or train? Ever make a phone call and work on the computer simultaneously or read a story to one child while bathing another? Say you're on a company softball team. Do you talk just about the game while you're sitting in the dugout, or are you discussing business, too? And when you perform your nightly bathroom routine, have you been known to brush your teeth while waiting for your facial mask to dry, just to save a few minutes?

All these acts may give you a certain sense of satisfaction at having accomplished a lot in a short amount of time—and sometimes, that's just what we need. The problem is, by mushing together all these tasks, we rarely come away feeling any sense of accomplishment at the way we completed any individual one. For instance, I can finish the crossword puzzle in the Sunday *New York Times* in ink while watching *ER*—but I'll make a lot of mistakes along the way before coming to the right solutions, leaving the grid looking like a giant scribble.

That's why spirituality demands that we stop at least once in a while to examine whether all our rushing about is worth it. We don't get many second chances in life; are we going to be happy having accomplished a lot, yet not having put our minds and hearts into any of it? Put it another way: In prayer, we give ourselves completely over to the act of communicating with God. Why can't we do the same thing with more mundane matters? Couldn't that be a form of divine communication, too?

And when we perform an act mindfully—be it meditating, vacuuming or playing Scrabble with a child—we nourish ourselves, as well. Rather than scattering our concentration on a dozen things at once, we focus. We slow down. We give ourselves time to calm down from the inside out and the luxury of saying: *Nothing is more important right now than this moment, this deed.* We may not get as much done by day's end, but we can feel more peaceful and satisfied with the work itself. That's a good way to think of it: Mindfulness is quality time for the soul.

Don't worry; I'm not going to ask you to become totally mindful of every step you take (unless you're taking your contemplative walk, which comes later on). But at least three times this week, pick a familiar task or situation and give it your total focus.

Say you're fixing breakfast. Rather than slapping it together and gulping it down, think about each motion as you go. How does the kitchen look? How does the floor feel beneath your feet? Is the sun shining through the window, a breeze rustling the curtains?

If you're making scrambled eggs, hold the eggs in your hand for a moment before you break them. Feel the shape and smoothness. Observe the way the yolks yield to the tines of your fork and the way the pepper scatters when you sprinkle it on the mixture. Listen to the hiss of the pan. See if you can pinpoint the exact moment in which the eggs turn from liquid to solid, and then to the precise fluffy consistency you prefer.

Cut into a fresh grapefruit or orange and smell the fragrant spray that emerges. Admire the color of the fruit, the tiny liquid-filled sacs packed into each segment. Even if you're pouring out juice from a carton, do it slowly. Hold the glass to the light and think about the fruit being squeezed to yield just this portion.

It doesn't matter what you choose. Watch your toast browning. Listen to the cereal fall into the bowl. Smell the sour tang of your yogurt. Even heating up leftover pizza can be spiritual if you approach it correctly.

Then, of course, comes the next part—eating. Again, use all your senses. Smell the meal before you take the first bite. Taste the way the salty and sweet foods mingle in your mouth, try to distinguish the coffee from the milk stirred inside. Feel the temperatures, sensations and textures: crunchy, hot, dry, moist, soft, cool, liquid, creamy. Put your fork and spoon down between bites and concentrate on what you're chewing before going for another mouthful. Try to feel the food making its way down to your stomach and imagine the nutrients fueling your body for the morning. Above all, enjoy your breakfast from first bite to last.

Getting a little hungry now? Great.

Think of other mindful activities you could do: dusting; washing dishes; taking a bath; writing a report; walking the dog; working out; reading to a child; shopping for clothes (you'll probably come away with fewer impulse buys); playing touch football; raking leaves; painting a room; driving down a country road; in-line skating; doing laundry; straightening your desk; collecting shells on the beach; even going to bed. (If you think it's delicious to snuggle under the covers now, wait until you're really aware of doing it.) A few of the other exercises in this book incorporate mindfulness, too.

Once you've completed your mindful task, you can go back to rushing around and doing nine things at once. But I'll bet it won't be as appealing anymore.

Talking to God
—and Making Him Listen

YOU PROBABLY KNEW this was going to come up sooner or later, so I'm going to start you on it this first week: Find a quiet moment every day and spend it in prayer.

It's easier than it sounds, and it's more important than you might think. Prayer gives us a perfect opportunity to get in touch with God (or the universe, if you prefer) and with ourselves. We can express gratitude, unburden ourselves, ask for what we want or simply say, "Here I am."

This is especially crucial for women, who tend to spend most of their time listening to other people and not enough time expressing what's in their own hearts. But men, traditionally expected to be self-reliant, also need the comfort and guidance that come from turning to God. When we do pour out our feelings, it's usually to a good friend, a husband, wife or partner—all of whom may be supportive and sympathetic, but who have problems of their own in the back of their minds that keep them from being absolutely there for us. (Admit it—haven't you ever tried to listen to a friend's complaints while at the same time putting a part of your brain to work figuring out what to do with the leftover rice in the fridge?)

No matter what we believe in, we need to be able to share the deepest part of ourselves, and a neutral Higher Power, who will listen nonjudgmentally and accept us for who we are, can be the best place to go for that catharsis.

There's no "bad" or "good" time to pray. There are as many times and ways to do it as there are minutes in the day, and you can do it as often as you like. For starters, though, I suggest picking a given time—that way, you'll be less likely to forget. I find that the more casual and individual the prayer, the better; as with any good relationship, you have to be fully yourself and feel trusted the way you are. Think of children just learning to pray, thanking God for everything from snow days to chocolate cake to getting the window seat. They beg for help—"Please, please, *please*!"—and even call on relatives who have passed on to intercede. Unselfconsciously, they ask for toys and blessings, talk about the unfairness of the world or tell God they don't want to talk to Him anymore.

That's exactly how you should approach your prayers. Get right in there. Be specific. Be grateful, be mad, be you. This will also prevent you from allowing your prayers to become droning recitations. Would you talk to your best friend about the same thing, using exactly the same words in the same way, every time? Of course not. You'd vary your conversation depending on what was on your mind at the moment. So it should be with prayer. As you change, so should your praying.

HERE ARE a few examples to get you on your way:

For the morning:

Good morning, God. Thank you for allowing me to rise to another day, and I'll try to make the most of the opportunities that come my way. This morning, I'm especially grateful for _____ and _____. But I'm also worried about _____ and _____. Please give me the strength to deal with these difficulties and whatever other ones may occur. Above all, help me to be true to my greatest self. Amen.

Before bed:

God, thank you for leading me safely through another day. I'm very grateful that _____ and _____ happened, but I wish _____ had turned out differently. I handled _____ challenge well, and I hope always to meet obstacles with grace and courage. Give me peace of mind, a night of rest for my mind and spirit and let me rise tomorrow renewed to face the new day. Amen.

To express gratitude:

God, who is like you? You have given me life, put me on earth filled with inexpressible beauty, surrounded me with family, friends, teachers, healers, animal companions, music, literature, art, science, wisdom and all the human mind can comprehend. Help me to continue to appreciate all that life has to offer, to see the little miracles as well as the bigger ones, to realize Your power and hand in all things and to help those who are in need of mental, physical or spiritual support. I hope to continue to grow in knowledge and compassion. Help me to realize, when I become too mired in my personal woes or too overwhelmed by outside pressures, that I am a part of a much greater whole, with an individual part to play. Help me realize that part. Thank you and amen.

Don't be afraid to express your less-than-positive emotions, either.

God, I'm so unhappy . . . I don't know when this pain is going to go away, and sometimes I wonder if you're even there, if you even care about my suffering. But I also know that without sorrow, there can also be no joy. Help me to endure this and give me the courage to know that the worst of this will ease.

I'm so afraid. I don't know what's going to happen. Don't abandon me. I need you now.

I'm mad. No, I'm furious. I'm frustrated and angry, and I'm tired of feeling this way. Nothing's going right. Why do these things happen to me? I'm mad at the world, at everyone—and at You, too, by the way. Make it stop. Help me get through this!

IF YOU'D RATHER communicate with God in a more familiar way, you can use a traditional prayer from your own faith or from another—Judaism, Hinduism, Islam, Native American supplications. The important point is that your prayer be as individual as you are.

Can you expect instant answers to your prayers? Answers, yes. Instant, maybe. Certainly not always. Some answers you have to look for. Some don't come for a while. Some aren't the answers you were hoping for. But I personally like this meditation: "Who rise from prayer better persons, their prayers are answered."

I've always thought of God as a pretty nice guy—not one of those stern parents, but somebody you could come to with open arms, who'd always listen. I talk to Him all the time: aloud if nobody's around and I've got something to say; otherwise, just in my head.
—VALERIE KALFRIN

I try praying for about ten minutes a night in bed. I began doing this more often after I was going through a period of personal pain about eight years ago. It was late at night and I was agonizing about a particular issue, and

I prayed for some peace—not a resolution of the issue that was causing me pain, but just some peace from the pain it was causing. Almost immediately, I felt peaceful and calm about the issue. (The next day, of course, I went back to worrying about it, but for that night, I was able to sleep.)

Since then, I have relied on prayer as a sort of relaxation technique. Sometimes it doesn't work; many times it does. It also allows me to take inventory of my life: areas I want to improve; people who need more love.
—LYNN COWAN

Two Christmases ago, I received as a gift Mother Teresa's book, A Simple Path, *which had several chapters devoted to prayer. I like attending church; however, laziness had gotten the better of me, and I hadn't been to Mass in some time. In the spring of the next year, I picked up the book and really concentrated on praying, meditation and being alone with myself.*

Each night, I would kneel down next to my bed. My room was completely dark and deafeningly silent. I would say the "Our Father" over and over, concentrating on every word. The experience was overwhelming. It is amazing how good it feels to really pray. I would be reduced to happy tears every night. It was a truly cathartic and stress-relieving feeling.

Needless to say, I was able to filter through the day's thoughts to get what was really important. I made the decisions I needed to make, and I truly believe that (1) they

were the right ones and (2) I would not have been able to feel so confident in my decisions if I had not prayed.
—JENNIFER WIGGINS

My prayers are often for my family and friends. When I pray for them and my prayers are answered, I know that God has been listening. When I pray for myself, I say the rosary or just have a dialogue with God. Even though my prayers may not be answered at that time, I know that I am being heard and will be helped at some future time.

Prayer has given me contentment and inner peace. I always feel calmer and more relaxed afterward. By continuing to pray every day, I am building a more meaningful relationship with God.
—GENEVIEVE O'HARE

Listening to God

YOUR NEXT ASSIGNMENT is to meditate once a day.

"Hold on!" I hear you cry. "I'm already committed to praying—isn't that the same thing?"

Well, no. There's a big difference. In prayer, we're actively communicating with the Power outside ourselves: asking, wishing, hoping, demanding. Meditation requires us to do just the opposite—to be still, clear our minds of thoughts and desires and let the universe speak to us.

Many of the exercises in here are very active ways of connecting with God—seeking Him in everyday activities and pleasures, through our senses, through natural creations. What we don't do often enough is stop running around in that frantic search and let God come to us. In that sense, I like to think about God in the familiar parent role. We're like toddlers let loose in a park, eager to experience everything and so caught up in ourselves that we tune out our parent's warnings and instructions. Only after we've expended our energy and are ready to sit quietly do we suddenly realize that our parent has been there all along, waiting for us. We turn our attention there, more willing now to hear what this parent—this great being so much older and wiser than us—has to say.

In addition to being a lesson in listening, meditation has proven health benefits, too. Dr. Herbert Benson of the Mind/Body Institute in Boston has found that patients who use his Relaxation Response to meditate report less stress, lower blood pressure, a reduction in feelings of depression and a bolstered immune system. Just as our bodies need rest to repair themselves, so do our minds need time away from conscious thinking to run at full capacity.

Meditation can be done anytime and anywhere, though it's best to find a time when you're not feeling rushed and won't be interrupted. Get up a few minutes before everyone else or go to bed a little later. If you're lucky enough to work in an office with a door, shut yourself in briefly during your lunch hour. Or go out and find a tree to sit under. If you're shopping alone, don't get out of the car right away—just sit in the parking lot and let yourself relax. (You might find yourself less apt to make impulse purchases afterward.)

Sit in a comfortable position on your bed, floor or chair. Inhale deeply through your nose, feeling your stomach rise up and out, then exhale through your mouth as your stomach sinks back in. (Many people do just the opposite, which is actually incorrect and doesn't allow for proper blood circulation and oxygenation. Ask any singer.) Do this four or five times. Check your body for any tense areas. Are your shoulders tensed up above your neck? Drop them. Are your hands clenched? Relax them. How about your jaw, your back, your legs?

You may want to meditate by repeating a calming word or phrase aloud, the way Dr. Benson recommends in his Relaxation Response. Try some words out for size until you come across one that feels right for you: *Om, Our Father, My Jesus, mercy, Shema Yisrael, amen, peace, calm, ocean.* I personally like *shalom*—if you draw it out, you have the hushed sound of *sh*, the "relief" syllable of *aaah*, and the *om* which we associate with Eastern spiritualism, plus the fact that "shalom" means "peace" gives it even more significance.

Repeat the word(s) over and over for a few minutes. Don't worry if they sound silly or meaningless; just be mindful of the sound and of your speaking. Naturally, since the brain is always on the go, intrusive thoughts will jump in there as you meditate. Probably more than one, and more than one at a time. When that happens, just acknowledge that the thought is there, then let it go and return to the meditation. If more unbidden thoughts pop in, do it again. Do it as often as you need to until your session is over.

It's going to seem frustrating at first, but don't give up. You'll be surprised at what happens when you keep at it. If nothing else, you'll come away calmer and more centered—and who wouldn't want that? But there can be other rewards, too.

I find that when I meditate, I get a wonderful sense of being surrounded by a safe, comforting presence. There's an energy there that I can almost touch if I try—but I keep still anyway, not wanting to interfere with the current. I don't receive specific spiritual messages often, but when I do, they're always positive ones that support my heart. Recently, while in a moment of quiet meditation, I felt a sense that something was telling me: *You know what you need to know.* Whether this came from somewhere in my subconscious mind or was inspired by something greater than myself, I found it very reassuring. At the time, I was overwhelmed with new responsibilities and wondering how long it would take for me to feel competent again. But feeling this message within me and thinking about its meaning—the knowledge I had was exactly what I needed at the moment—was like a booster shot of self-confidence. I came away from that session feeling as though I could conquer the world.

You may not end every meditation feeling the same way, but you'll be calmer and more at peace with yourself and your surroundings. That's not just a spiritual feeling— that's a pretty nice way to go through life, too.

I meditate at least twice a week. I light a scented candle (somehow, that just helps), play some soft music and listen. Meditation is my way of taking time out of the day to listen to the Lord. I just let in whatever comes to mind. I find that after a while, my mind clears and I come up with solutions to problems that I never thought

possible before. I know this is the Lord's way of showing me that when we take time to listen to Him, he will always take the time to listen to us.
   —TOYA SMITH

One day in yoga class, after clearing my head and trying to focus on "my" God, I found myself looking inward. I felt an incredible sense of peace come over me. I'm not sure why I became so introspective. It's not like I've never been to church or temple. I don't even think I could find God if I looked.
   Oh . . . maybe he's in me?
   —JENNIFER MCCORMICK

Being a bit of a "Type A" personality, I find it very difficult to sit still for very long without doing something—be it reading, tuning in to the news or tracking the latest movie memorabilia auctions on the Internet. My first few attempts at meditating were failures. Sitting anywhere in the vicinity of books, magazines or electrical appliances, even with my eyes closed, created too much temptation to stray from perfect quietude.
   The solution for me lay in modest deprivation. Every other morning, I shut myself into my windowless bathroom after breakfast and perched cross-legged on a pillow in the tub with a candle on the sink. This helped deaden any street sounds. At first I focused on the candle flame, then gradually I closed my eyes and let myself drift into relaxation. My breathing slowed, deepened—

respiration became something to be savored rather than taken for granted. Amid the general mind-clearing, creative thoughts about a current writing endeavor (and possible new projects) formed—the sort of free association of ideas and informational fragments that usually occurs on that pleasurable threshold between wakefulness and sleep's welcoming embrace.

Interestingly, some of my more fascinating thoughts dissipated when I broke from meditation. What remained were what I can describe only as velvet patches of comfort that formed a stress-deflecting quilt for the rest of the day.

I began taking a more measured approach to my chores and business. Where once I would sit at my home office desk and fret over an eternal pile of files and adhesive notes, wondering what to do first, I found myself chipping away steadily at the work and making necessary phone calls without the usual panicky edge.

—DEAN LAMANNA

Listening to Your Soul

MY LATEST OBSESSION is visiting Web sites. It's hard to believe that we managed to exist without the Internet for so long, and now that it's available, the possibilities are limitless. Whatever your interest or problem—pets, pregnancy, careers, books, basketball, diabetes, music, amusement parks, etiquette, religion, dating, European restaurants—you'll find any number of kindred spirits with whom to share ideas and opinions.

But what I like best is going to Web sites for women and looking for message boards in which members write in, asking for advice on their questions and problems. It's amazing how much we reveal under the safe cover of anonymity and how eagerly we reach out to people we don't know, asking them to judge their actions or guide them to a decision.

"Should I marry this man?" they say. "Should I leave this job?" "Is this friendship over?" "Do I have the talent to write a book?" "Why can't I get a date?" "Do I have to invite these people?" "Could this lump be cancer?" "Am I going to the wrong church?" "I'm pregnant—what should I do?" "How can I keep my child safe from bullies?" "I feel so sad . . . what could be wrong?"

All difficult issues, to be sure. But if you've ever read any of these message-board posts, you know that the people who write them very rarely ask a one-sentence question and leave it at that. No, they're more likely to include a lot of background information about themselves and describe their particular situation in minute detail. They want to be sure you know where they're coming from.

What's really interesting, though, is that most of the time, these writers aren't as confused as they appear at first sight. Often, their posts reveal that they already know the answer to their question. They're just looking for someone to validate what they already know. You'll see statements like: "He's separated, and he says he doesn't love her anymore, but he doesn't want to file for divorce until his children are a little older. Should I wait for him?" Or: "My doctor says everything's normal, but something just doesn't feel right. Am I being neurotic?" Or: "I've always wanted to be an actor, but it's crazy to quit my job for a long-shot dream like that, right?"

Many computer users reading these posts may wonder why some people can't bring themselves to trust the answer that's already nestled in their hearts. Sometimes the writers responding to these questions sound downright frustrated: "Leave him already!" "Find another doctor now!" "You only go around once in life—why not find a way to make your dream come true?"

But we're all guilty of ignoring our better judgment. I've tried to convince myself that a dress looks good on me in the dressing room, only to have it sit in the closet for months after bringing it home. I've reached for candy bars that I didn't even want and regretted it later once I hit the gym. And I can't begin to count the number of times I've said yes to a favor or a task, even when I could literally hear my brain screaming, *No! No! No!*

Call it self-awareness, a sixth sense, intuition, conscience, gut feelings, the "still small voice"—those unspoken messages we receive all come from the deep part of our souls that keeps alert to everything we do and knows what actions are appropriate for us as individuals. It's one of the things that sets us apart from the rest of the animals, and as such can be both a blessing and a curse. Like it or not, we're accountable for what we do when we listen to our souls and when we don't.

Yet all too often, we ignore those internal signals, stubbornly telling ourselves that what we're doing is right, even when our soul tells us otherwise. *I can do this, we think. It'll be okay. I'll make it right. He'll change. She doesn't need me. There's got to be a light somewhere at the end of the tunnel.*

The strange part is that when we don't trust our soul's messages, we're surprised when things go wrong. Odder still, more often than not we go on to ignore that little nagging voice when it pipes up yet again!

Sometimes our soul has to pass the word along to our bodies before we're willing to listen and learn from what it has to say. You tack too many activities and responsibilities onto your schedule, and next thing you know, you're fighting off the flu. You stay in that dead-end job and wonder why you feel angry and weepy on Sunday night. You say yes to someone you're not sure you really love, and in the middle of the wedding gown fitting, your heart starts to race and your head goes woozy.

If you pick only one exercise in this book to follow, make it this one: Listen to your soul. At the risk of sounding like that embarrassingly sappy song about the all-knowing "tiny scout" from *An Affair to Remember*, I'll say it again: Listen to your soul.

You already know what that voice sounds like. Whenever you've felt called to do or choose something— or felt that some power was leading you away from an action or a decision—you were following the dictates of your heart. Every cell in your body felt pushed toward the answer, and if you went against that instinct, there was a gnawing feeling of doubt that probably never left you completely.

But for the purposes of this exercise, we'll start small. You won't have to ask your soul for guidance on anything earth-shattering. Three times this week, take a simple yes-or-no choice—*Shall I have pasta for dinner? Will I buy the new Jewel CD now or wait till Christmas? Will I have sex tonight? Will I call my mother?*—and sit down with your soul until you have an answer.

Go into your room and make yourself comfortable. Then pose the question to your soul and wait. Sometimes the answer that feels right will come to you right away, if not, then try thinking about each possibility and see what comes up. Does any part of your body feel tense or uncomfortable when you think about a certain choice? Does your heart feel heavy or peaceful?

If you like, imagine your soul as a light or a being living in a deep, warm, safe place inside you. Talk to it as you would to a friend. Trust it. What is it telling you? If you still have trouble coming up with an answer that feels right, imagine that you're reading the question on a message board. What would you tell that person?

A word of warning: Don't confuse soul messages with guilt, and avoid phrasing your question in the form of "should I" or "could I." Many times, we make choices that feel wrong to us because we feel obligated or pressured, or because we think it ought to be the "right thing" to do. Unless your heart of hearts is urging you that something you "should" do feels right, you'll only be punishing yourself. For instance, one evening you might debate about whether to bring home work from the office or to leave it and take a calming aromatherapy bath instead. Everything within you is dying to have that long soak, but you take the work home instead because you ought to do it, it's important, your career should come first. By the time you're ready for bed, you're no less exhausted and stressed than you were at work. If you had listened to your soul, you might have been more relaxed from that bath and ready to face the work back in the office the next day.

On the other hand, there may be times when your soul really will feel peaceful at the thought of bringing home work at night. Maybe it's a high-profile project that could win you a promotion or raise. Or it could be a task that you can accomplish more quickly in the quiet of your house. Or perhaps it's not an assignment you enjoy, but you know that once it's done, a weight will lift from your shoulders. What's important isn't necessarily the choice itself, but how it makes you feel inside.

This is just another way in which you can learn to live with awareness. The better you know yourself—and that means the inner reaches as well as the outer appearance—the more confident you'll be when it comes not only to making decisions, but also to your marriage or social life, parenting, working, playing and just *being*. Not to mention the fact that opening yourself up to your soul makes it so much easier to open up to God. It's much easier to fill up an open container than a closed one.

Visiting God at Home

ONE DAY this weekend, your assignment is to attend a house of worship.

This may already be an established part of your life, in which case, this will be an easy exercise. But if you don't already go, do it at least once—even if the idea of organized religion turns you off. You don't have to go to the church or temple you grew up with. You can even try one from a different denomination altogether. But please try it.

The idea here isn't to make you feel uncomfortable or force you to adhere to one faith. But within the structures of religious services, there are elements that you can take and apply to your life elsewhere. There's prayer, of course. But there's often music, too. There are images, sounds, scents and tastes. There's the atmosphere of awe and holiness. There are sacred texts and the lessons they teach us; symbols of things we hold dear. There's personal reflection and the call to become true to our best selves.

When I first started attending Friday night services at the synagogue I eventually joined, the one thing that struck me immediately was the deep sense of peace I felt. Closed off from the working world and reading psalms with their evocative imagery, I could allow a part of myself to open up and take it all in. Since then, I look for ways to find that inner stillness even if I'm not worshipping.

And though the pageantry of the Catholic services I sometimes attend with my husband is unfamiliar, I find beauty in the music, hundreds of years old; in the faces of parishioners taking Communion and feeling a personal connection to God; and in the sign of peace, in which strangers and relatives alike become, just for a moment, part of the entire family of man.

Even the simplest of rites can be deeply meaningful. In Quaker meeting houses, there is no group prayer, singing or sermons. Worshippers simply sit in a respectful silence, then rise on a voluntary basis to talk about whatever may be in their hearts.

But one of the most important aspects of group worship is that it is done as a community. There's a basic human need to be in the company of others, to connect in mind and heart and to work together toward common goals. Though we may be worshipping in our own ways and asking for purely self-oriented things, there is a comfort in doing it as part of a larger team. Although many rituals we perform to enhance our spiritual selves are done alone, it's not possible to be a completely spiritual person by shutting away the rest of the world all of the time.

If you're so inspired, try attending both a service of the religion you know best and one that's less familiar to you. Most houses of worship welcome visitors to their regular weekly services, and you'll gain an even greater appreciation of the many ways in which people connect with their Higher Power. You might find it more interesting to attend a service that's considerably different from your own. For instance, if you're Presbyterian, try a synagogue, a Hindu temple or even a charismatic Christian church.

Call ahead to find out days and times and ask about any visitor restrictions. In some cases, visitors seated separately sit apart from the rest of the congregation; some religions (such as Islam and Orthodox Judaism) require women to sit apart from men and to dress modestly. But you don't need to recite the prayers or songs if you don't feel comfortable doing so or to contribute if an offertory is made. In churches where Communion is offered, guests may be restricted from taking it; again, ask first before the service.

Once you've had a taste of how other faiths worship, you might find it interesting to find a friend, colleague or relative who practices a different religion and ask her about her beliefs. If you know a Buddhist, you could discuss whether this is his family's religion or whether he came to it on his own—and why. Ask what role Buddha plays in the faith, what the main tenets of Buddhism are, the meaning of the major holidays, of reincarnation. Find out what makes the religion meaningful to him.

While you're in the service, pay special attention to

whatever moves you. Is it the words? The music? The joy? The rituals or symbols? The quiet? The people? Make note of it afterward. Once you know what makes you feel more in tune with God, it'll be easier for you to find other ways to experience those emotions and thoughts. Many of the other assignments in this book come back to these basic concepts.

Even if you come away from this exercise not especially inclined to go to services every week, you'll at least have learned something about why other people worship together, and you'll understand more about your own sense of spirituality.

Your Spiritual Journal

REMEMBER that diary you kept when you were younger? If you're like me, you probably still have it somewhere—that well-worn, well-loved notebook or leatherette-bound tome in which you confided your deepest secrets and desires: "My parents are sooo unfair!" "When will Craig realize that I'm alive and madly in love with him?" "I hate the world." "I got my period yesterday . . . I guess I'm really a woman now."

Sometimes you wrote about things you couldn't even tell your best friend about: the crushes, the fears, the loneliness. It was a nonjudgmental listener whom you could trust never to reveal the workings of your heart. When you think about it, keeping a diary isn't all that far removed from praying—and sometimes better, in a way. Very often, the emotions expressed on those pages are more sincere and heartfelt than the rote passages we chant in church.

Since you're probably familiar with the habit of keeping a journal, then this next exercise should be fairly easy: You're going to start keeping a diary of all the spiritual moments that happen to you every day.

Though it might seem a little much to write about spiritual things in addition to communicating with God, this is just as important an exercise as sitting in meditation. Spiritual moments are all around us, but frequently, we let them go by unnoticed. After a while, we start going through our daily routines without realizing the ways in which we are being touched by God. But when you sit down to write about these events, they fix themselves in your mind and heart more readily than if you let them go unrecorded. Knowing that you'll be called upon to make these journal entries will not only make you more aware of them, but you'll also start consciously looking for them. You'll probably find that your later entries are considerably longer than your earlier ones.

So now it's time to get started. Find a notebook, blank book or scrapbook that appeals to you: small or large, lined or unlined. Even a pad of looseleaf is fine, as long as you keep the pages together—you don't want to lose half the journal all over the house. Get a writing implement that you're comfortable with—whether it's a number 2 pencil, a plain ballpoint or a fancier fountain pen. I have a friend who used to love those super-fine felt-tip pens you see in stationery stores, preferably in lavender or green. She just felt freer expressing herself with them. That's how you should feel with the pen you use. If you're too techno-savvy to use anything but a computer, go ahead. But save your work to a disk reserved just for your journal.

Once you have the book that's right for you, put it in a spot where you'll be sure to see it easily. It's too easy to slip a notebook in a drawer and forget about it. A desk or nightstand is preferable. Commit yourself to writing in it every night, even if it's only for a couple of minutes. Try it just before you go to bed. (That goes for computer users, too.)

So what do you write about? What constitutes a spiritual moment? That's the easy part: It's whatever you decide touches your soul and makes you feel more connected to God. It could be a church or temple service. A single prayer. Lighting a candle. Singing a hymn. Keeping your daily silence. Reading a favorite passage from a book.

Write about natural events, like a thunderstorm or the sudden quiet that comes after it. Watching a river flow downstream or waves crashing against the shore. A brilliant sunset changing from orange to pink to deep blue. A bird building its nest. The first crocuses pushing through the cold earth after a dreary winter. Even a disaster like a hurricane or an earthquake can be spiritual if it makes you aware of the force of God's power. The moments don't always have to be cheery ones.

Write about human moments. There's the cozy warmth of sitting down to coffee with a good friend. The way a child laughs spontaneously or the awe in his eyes as you read him a bedtime story. The wonderful feeling of your loved one's skin or the contentment following the lovemaking. Those overwhelming surges of love that come at unexpected times. The gratitude you feel when someone does you a favor or the joy of doing something nice yourself.

Use your imagination and open yourself to the possibilities. For instance, my list for the day might include a walk I took with my husband in which we needed no words to understand each other; seeing the smile on my cat as he curls up on a doll quilt; the relaxation of my morning shower; the way I felt when I sat at my computer to write this book and watched the words come out of my fingers as if they were being written by someone else.

You might find it easier at first just to jot down your entries in simple list form: "Watched the snow fall; the smell of my baby after her bath; reading the Twenty-third Psalm and feeling God's protection; eating Mom's sumptuous chocolate cake; that dreamy swimming feeling I got just before falling asleep."

Then, once you've gotten into the rhythm of writing, try to expand on your entries. Think about how you felt during each of those moments and why you considered them spiritual. For example, when contemplating that cake, you could say, "Had a piece of Mom's chocolate cake left over from Dan's birthday . . . the richness rolling around my tongue made me grateful that I can taste and appreciate something so good. I felt the love that Mom put into it, knowing that it was Dan's favorite. It also made me aware that not everyone is fortunate enough to have cake at dinner—or even to have dinner at all. Let me be aware of the many blessings I take for granted. And thank God for chocolate—talk about a divinely inspired food!"

Every few weeks, go back and look through your earlier entries. You'll be surprised at how many things you've found to write about, but that's only a part of it. Do you notice any patterns? Are there themes that seem to come up day after day? If so, take note of them. They're messages from your soul that should alert you to the way in which you experience a connection with God. For instance, if your journal is filled with descriptions of sunsets, flowers and mountain breezes, then you clearly feel closest to God when you're outdoors. In that case, you'll want to take as many opportunities as possible to be out there admiring those wonders. Or if your entries are primarily centered on interactions with people, then you would look for other ways to make similar connections, such as calling old friends more often or doing volunteer work.

One final note about journaling: It's as true an expression of yourself as you'll ever leave on this earth. Some of the most famous works of world literature have been in journal form—from authors such as Samuel Pepys and Anne Frank. While you may not become as famous as they were, this journal will be a lasting tribute to your relationship to God and the world.

My first journal entry was a revelation. I think of myself as a sensitive, spiritually aware person, so I was surprised to find I didn't feel particularly connected. "Distant," I wrote. If God is watching me, He's doing so heavens away.

But as I started to look for that connectedness, I realized it really wasn't so distant, after all. At first, there was a bird on my daily walk. High in the sky, but still visible. Yes, I felt somehow connected. Day by day, the feeling grew stronger. Good things happened I hadn't expected. Bad things happened that needed to. And I realized: If there was anyone being distant, it wasn't God. It was me.

—CARLY PAULSEN

Several years ago, when we were having family problems, I complained that I was having great difficulty focusing on my prayer life, especially during crisis times when I needed it the most. Our family therapist suggested that I write my prayers down.

This changed my life. Since I'm a writer, I communicate best that way, and since I have such a busy life, filled with activities, work and obligations, I would often lose my focus when I prayed silently. So every morning, I write a letter to God. I first began with a fancy journal, but now I just fill legal pads, which are less expensive. After I finish pouring out my heart to God and thanking Him for my blessings, I then seek guidance and direction. It's amazing how clear my mind is after I pray. And when I'm going through a difficult time, it's hard, but writing allows me to pour my heart out and let the pain flow.

—SUSAN WALES

Congratulations—you've spent an entire week working on your spiritual side. Now take just a minute to reflect on what you did and how the exercises worked for you. Using this book or a separate piece of paper (or better yet, your journal), answer these questions as honestly as you can:

What did I learn this week?

What exercise did I enjoy most?   *Why?*

Was there an exercise that didn't work for me?

Why didn't it work?

Is there anything I could do to achieve the same result?

How do I feel about myself right now?

How do I feel about God?

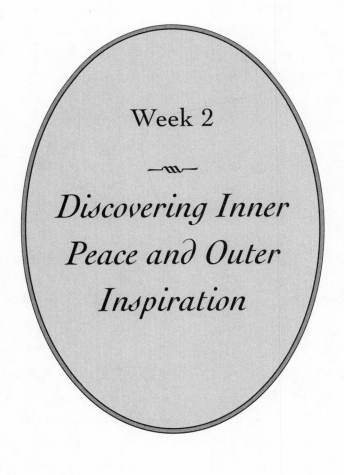

Week 2

Discovering Inner
Peace and Outer
Inspiration

This is going to be a quiet week for you. The exercises for the next seven days emphasize thought, introspection and silence—both the literal absence of sound and the quiet of the inner soul. God is in the quiet as well as the noise, between the lines as well as in the words, but most of the time, we're too busy making our own racket to pause and listen.

Continue, if you can, the daily practices from Week 1 that work best for you—prayer, meditation, journaling, mindfulness—while trying out these new reflective exercises. See for yourself how putting moments of calm in your day can make the rest of the time seem less hassled, too.

The Sounds of Silence

WHEN WAS THE LAST TIME you spent any length of time—apart from sleep, which doesn't count—in perfect silence? We're so used to having our ears filled with noise in every waking moment that it seems unnatural to be without it. We talk incessantly to our friends and colleagues, trying to fill in any awkward pauses. Throughout the day, we rely on all sorts of clicking, beeping, whirring and screeching devices to make our lives easier. Even at home alone, there's the temptation to turn on the TV and radio "for company." I know I often burst into song while doing dishes for no other reason than to fill in the dead air.

Quiet is scary. In the absence of sound, we're keenly aware of ourselves and our thoughts. We might even hear messages coming straight from our souls that we ordinarily try to drown out with car horns and Muzak.

But that's exactly why silence is such a highly spiritual concept. We observe "a moment of silence" at funerals and memorial services to honor the memory of the dead. We pray wordlessly in church and sing of the "silent night" that is considered one of the holiest in history. Some religious orders even require their members to spend most or all of their days in quiet, so that God can enter at will without having to cut through a tiresome stream of chatter.

Your next spiritual exercise is to spend at least fifteen minutes every day in absolute quiet. No talking. No music. No background noise loud enough to disturb your solitude. If that means getting up half an hour before anyone else or staying up a little later, so be it. The important thing is that the time be unrushed and calm. And because this is time for you and your thoughts, don't use it to read, write, rearrange the photos in your album or scrub the tub. (Soaking in it, however, is fine.)

Since this isn't a meditative time, you don't have to focus on a particular thought, prayer or request. Just sit quietly and let your thoughts come and go as they will. You may find a message coming to you, a wish, question or plea that seems to come from somewhere deep within. Pay attention to it. Is there something you need to do, a yearning that needs to be fulfilled?

Some days, all you'll feel is restlessness, boredom, fatigue or a hundred little thoughts scurrying around your head. That's okay, too. Just accept the thoughts and feelings as they come to you and keep yourself open to other possibilities.

You may find it uncomfortable at first. Solitude and

quiet are awesome, frightening things. But keep at it. You'll find that you are the only company you need. And the sounds that come from no sound at all are wondrous.

Finding ten minutes of silence in New York City can be a challenge. The first day, as I sat in the living room, I was distracted by the sounds of jets, cars and a child calling a dog. My cat, who considers any lap on the planet to be his, was insisting on sitting on mine. It was tough to maintain the silence and connect with my spiritual side. Work, play and life kept intruding.

I really didn't think I'd be able to complete the assignment—until one day, I had a breakthrough of a most unusual kind. After a particularly difficult day at work, I had some time to kill, so I decided to take my ten minutes on a bench on Fifth Avenue in Manhattan—not a place to find spirituality and silence. But here, at one of the world's busiest intersections, I was at peace. I found myself at some level different from any I'd ever been in before. Surrounded by heat and humidity, diesel fumes and wave after wave of tired, harried people, I had actually found the inner silence I was looking for.

I've found it ever since. Actively searching for perfect silence only makes the noise more distracting and annoying. The best thing to do is to let the silence come to you.
—JOHN O'HARE

Walking with Awareness

TODAY'S STOP on the road to inner spirituality is the contemplative walk. This is a deliberately carved-out piece of time that you'll use to calm yourself, gather your thoughts and become more peaceful with yourself.

The contemplative walk is wonderful because you can do it anywhere—in a quiet park, around your block, on a city street. It can be as long or as short as you like (though it should last at least fifteen minutes; less than that, and you'll be through before you really start to enjoy the benefits). You don't have to wear spandex shorts (very few people can wear them and feel calm walking in public); you can be in a business suit and still come away refreshed. But to truly be effective, aim to walk at least four times a week.

To begin, as the corporate slogan goes, just do it. Step outside and walk in whatever direction strikes your fancy that day. (You can walk indoors or on a treadmill if the weather's too bad, but the effect won't be the same.) Keep your pace steady, but not too brisk; this isn't a workout.

But above all, walk with awareness. Focus fully on all your senses: the feel of the ground under your feet; the way the sky looks and whose garden is growing; the smells you encounter, be they honeysuckle, sun-warmed grass or the aroma of grilled hot dogs from the vending cart. You might taste this morning's coffee on your tongue or the humidity in the air.

Breathe deeply as you go and feel your breath going in and out. Notice your heart pumping and the muscles in your legs contracting. Think about being here on this earth, in this moment, fitting precisely into the space you're in, open to everything around you. Imagine yourself becoming more peaceful with every step.

Try not to think about anything in particular except the walking, the environment and your soul becoming calmer. If a problem or disturbing thought passes through your mind, acknowledge it and let it go. And if you walk with a partner or friend, don't talk to each other; that will cut into your awareness. Just enjoy each other's company and focus on your own serenity.

A contemplative walk can be taken any time of day or whenever you feel you need it most. I try to fit it into my lunch hour whenever possible; I find that I come back much more prepared to face phone calls, meetings and heavy editing jobs. But if your first reaction to this exercise was: "What is she, nuts? How can I possibly find the time to go for a walk and do nothing?," then maybe it's time to ask yourself why you're putting all your other priorities ahead of your own well-being. A contemplative walk is meant to be a break from the routine, to rejuvenate body and soul, just to *be*. It's a prayer that you give to yourself. Oh, the job and the kids and the crises will still be there when you get back from your walk. You'll just be able to cope with them more easily.

I live just half a block from the southern California beach. I started modestly, with a total round trip of about a mile, then gradually worked up to about twice that distance. The walks proved a perfect supplement for my meditations, with similar de-stressing results: general head-clearing and, especially, deeper breaths.

For me, few places can inspire beautiful awe and a sense of something well beyond our comprehension at work, than a shoreline (though the mountains and desert come very close). It is the place where the Big Three of the natural environment—the earth, sea and sky—come together in a visual and aural symphony. It is a harmonic convergence that keeps the size of humanity in strict perspective while delivering all of the sensations that can amp up an individual's aliveness quotient. It is also a reminder that there are other inhabitants of this planet coping with their existence the best they know how.

A perfect illustration of this came about midway through the third week of my beach strolls, when I encountered a baby sea lion sprawled below a dune several yards above the tide line. At first I thought that perhaps it was injured, so I slowly approached to investigate. But the very sharp bark it cast in my direction had only one message: "Pardon me, but you're disturbing my quiet time!"

Every living thing needs its space. And by taking the time each day to keep up with my own spiritual maintenance, I'm less likely to bark in any situation.

—DEAN LAMANNA

(Spiritual) Reading Is
Fundamental

IF YOU'VE EVER BEEN to a synagogue, you'll remember the portion of the service in which the Torah is taken out of the ark as the congregation rises to their feet. The rabbi walks through the aisles, carrying the scrolls, while everyone touches their prayer books or tallits (prayer shawls) to the Torah cover in a gesture of respect. When the weekly reading is completed, the rabbi holds the Torah high above his or her head so that the congregants can see the ancient words and pronounces, "This is the Torah that Moses placed before the people of Israel to fulfill the word of God."

Although I was hardly a devout Jew when I was growing up (as you know by now), the one thing I did understand was the significance of the Torah ceremony. I've been a voracious reader since I was three years old, so the idea of a book being so sacred that it had to be dressed in velvet covers and put in a special case seemed natural to me. Since the book had special stories in it, it was only logical that we should honor it and read it aloud. Part of the reason I chose not to have my bat mitzvah ceremony at thirteen was because I knew what an honor it was to be asked to read from the scrolls. Since I wasn't especially involved in my religion at the time, it didn't seem right to allow myself that particular privilege.

Still, my earlier experience had taught me that it was possible—and very desirable—to find inspiration through the written word. Over the years, I went on to do just that. Through my own discoveries and through friends' recommendations, I was introduced to authors such as Rabbi Harold Kushner, Madeleine L'Engle, Hugh Prather, Kathleen Norris, Joan Borysenko and Iyanla Vanzant. Others showed me the simple wisdom in old childhood favorites like *The Little Prince* and *The Velveteen Rabbit*. When I began studying for my bat mitzvah, I read commentary on the Torah and books on Jewish spirituality. I even began to tackle the Torah itself (slowly). Now one of my goals in the new millennium is to delve more deeply into books that play a part in other religious traditions.

Sacred texts are a crucial part of every faith, whether they're as ancient as the Bhagavad Gita or as current as the Book of Mormon. Through them we learn, think, question, teach, enlighten and guide ourselves closer to the people we most want to be. We use them to gain a better understanding of God and His place in our lives. We empathize with the all-too-human characters in the stories and realize how little has changed since then. We use them to become better people. There's a saying in Judaism that the study of Torah is equal to such *mitzvot* (commandments) as honoring parents, doing deeds of loving-kindness, making peace, welcoming strangers, rejoicing with bride and groom, visiting the sick and comforting the bereaved, because it naturally leads the student to perform all these acts.

Then there's the fact that the very act of reading takes us out of ourselves and the workaday world. As Emily Dickinson put it, books are the "frigate" that carries us to a realm of thought, wonder and knowledge. I'm sure I don't need to sell you on the idea of reading as a stress-buster; who hasn't come home after a tough day and collapsed with an escapist novel or stayed up late to finish just one more chapter?

So this next assignment should be an easy one to tackle. Every day for the rest of the week, read at least a small portion of a book you find inspirational.

By "inspirational," I mean a book that either makes you feel closer to your concept of God or one whose message moves you to better yourself in some way. But be honest with yourself. You may be a huge fan of romance novels, technothrillers or vampire tales, and there's nothing wrong with that—except that few people would argue that they were written with the intent of making readers feel spiritually fulfilled. So read these books all you like; just be sure to put aside some time for more soul-enriching works, as well.

Some of you may already be reading the Bible every day. If you do, that's great; you might want to find another title and add that to your daily reading, too. If not, a religious text is certainly a good place to start, be it the Bible, the Talmud, the Koran or the Tao Te Ching. Or try one of the current bestselling spiritual writers, such as Deepak Chopra, M. Scott Peck, Richard Bach, Timothy Jones, Iyanla Vanzant, Adin Steinsalz or any of the other authors on the ever-overflowing inspirational shelves. (No, this book doesn't count—but thank you!) If *The Prophet*, poetry or a children's classic inspire you, keep a copy close at hand.

I find that it's easiest to keep to a daily reading habit if I put a book on my bedstand and pick it up just before I go to sleep. But if you'd rather do your reading first thing in the morning, in your office before lunch or in the kitchen while everyone else watches TV in the family room, that's fine. Just give yourself enough time to really enjoy what you're reading and enough quiet to allow yourself space to think.

Be sure to read each sentence—each word, for that matter—carefully. Let your eyes and mind savor them. Stop every once in a while and think about what the book's messages mean to you. What rings true? What can you learn? How might you apply the principles you've just read when you go to work tomorrow or deal with the children?

You don't necessarily have to agree with everything your book says, and you probably won't, especially if you're reading something unfamiliar or from a religious tradition different from your own. But this can be a valuable lesson in self-awareness. Instead of dismissing an idea with "That can't be right," think about why you're disagreeing. How does it conflict with your beliefs? Take a look at the credo you wrote. Does it say something totally different from the message in the book? How would you respond to the author if you could meet him or her in person?

Don't automatically agree with everything in your book, either. Remember the chapter you just read on listening to your soul. Does every page, every instruction, every moral feel right, deep down where it counts? If not, why not? Again, go back to your credo. Don't be afraid to wonder or question. Questioning doesn't kill faith—it enriches faith.

You probably won't finish your entire book this week, but take as much as you can out of it. If you want to continue reading for the rest of the month, so much the better. That goes for all of the exercises here. If any of them appeal to you so much that you want to carry on beyond the recommended time frame, don't let me stop you! That means you've found something that really resonates within. You're discovering what it takes for you to develop a comfortable relationship with your soul and a connection to the greater good beyond.

I found my prayers becoming somewhat mindless and mechanical—wasting God's time as well as mine. Seeking inspiration for my prayer time, I turned to the saints for guidance. First, I tried to think of a particular saint who was renowned for prayer, but St. Francis was the only one I could remember. Realizing how little I remembered from Confirmation *preparation class, I was spurred on to pick up a copy of* The Lives of the Saints.

Reading the biographies, I was amazed at how many of their experiences I could apply to my own life. Although the vast majority of them lived long before my time, many things about humankind have remained the same. The challenges they faced are the same we face today, especially as adults.

Since the book I have is arranged by feast days, I've made it a daily devotional. Before I start, I make the sign of the cross, ask for guidance on what I'm about to read and the ability not only to understand the material but also how the events of the saint's life relate to my own. Then I read the passage for the day slowly and carefully, really thinking about the material, and pray the short prayer provided at the end of the biography.

I try to integrate the attitudes or teachings of each saint into the day. For example, St. John Vianney was known for his patience—and I'm a very impatient person. I'll never be as saintly as he was, but I tried to be a little more patient that day. Then before I went to bed, I asked God to help me curb my impatience, as well as to help those who may be hurt by it. I didn't wake up the next morning the very soul of patience, but it made me aware of this particular shortcoming. (A little humility never hurt anybody.) The experience was very empowering, making me aware of how much control I have over my life if I choose.

—TRACY TIDINGS-AMUNDSEN

Finding the Charm in Music

TODAY'S ASSIGNMENT is almost deceptively simple: Listen to music that you find spiritually uplifting. By this, I mean music that grabs you by the heart, burrows its way through your soul, sends your spine shivering and leaves you both thoroughly cleansed and yearning for more at the same time.

Go ahead and look through your CD collection now. Play some selections until you find a few that satisfy you the way no other works can. For me, Beethoven's Ninth never fails to set my spirit soaring. You might prefer Mozart or Handel or Vivaldi. Or maybe it's jazz that gets you jazzed. Salsa that rings through your body. Old-fashioned gospel or today's pop inspirational singers. The hypnotic patterns of Eastern music—sitar, takahashi. Sinatra or Alanis or Enya or Boyz 2 Men.

Then take ten or fifteen minutes out of your day, pop in the album and cue up the piece, sit in a comfortable place, close your eyes and listen.

And do nothing else.

That's the tricky part.

Music has become so much a part of our daily routine—from the Muzak that plays while our call is on hold to the disco that blares during aerobics class to the soft rock piped in at the supermarket—that we treat it like background noise even as we pretend to be listening. You're not really feeling the notes when you're in another room making the bed or when you put on headphones to run on the treadmill or even when you're dancing at a party.

So this is your time to listen to the music for its own sake. Two or three times a week, find an album or song that truly inspires you, then shoo everyone else out of the room while you put it on. Get comfortable, close your eyes and listen.

Concentrate on the notes as they happen. Don't try to anticipate the next chord or chorus. Enjoy the tones while they're still fresh in your ears. Try listening to first one instrument, then another. Does any one of them move you more deeply than the others? Which says more to you—a saxophone or a trumpet? An electric guitar or an acoustic one? To me, for instance, a piano expresses the drama and excitement I can't always formulate in words, and even the most upbeat violin pieces seem to me to have an underlying sweet sadness that moves me deeply.

As you listen, relax your body from your head on down. Check yourself for tense spots, then consciously loosen those muscles. Nothing should distract you from hearing the music, least of all hunched-up shoulders or clenched hands. (Just don't get so relaxed that you fall asleep!)

Then imagine that there's a direct line from your ears down through your neck and into your heart. See the music working its way through your body and pay attention to the emotions that come up. Does this piece make you feel elated? Sad? Inspired? Yearning for something? Let the feelings happen as they will; don't fight the tears or suppress a giggle.

When the song or sonata or symphony is over, feel free to play it again if you feel you need the extra time to process it fully. But I recommend choosing different songs or styles of music each time you give yourself a musical session. This will keep the exercise from becoming too routine, and you'll be better able to draw something new from the music every time.

This is also a great opportunity to try out new musical genres and discover whether they move you spiritually. If you're a die-hard country fan, try trading your Garth and Dixie Chicks for Mozart one day. If your collection is mostly classical, try a gospel tune instead. See if your library has traditional African music, Celtic instrumentals, cantors singing Jewish liturgy, the chants of Hildegard of Bingen. Or explore different styles within the music you like: Aretha Franklin, Billie Holiday, John Coltrane, 'N Sync, Hank Williams, Schubert. Music is a form of prayer, and there are as many styles of inspirational music as there are ways to pray.

Remember to note in your journal the music that fills you spiritually and note how it makes you feel. Then see whether you can find other moments in your life that make you feel that same breathless joy or pangs of sorrow. Again, this is all intended to help you hear what your soul is saying. Once you know its messages and triggers, the easier it will be for you to experience that same sensation while going about your daily life.

I attend church services every week. I love the music, both hearing it and singing along. When I leave the services, I've always got the last song we sang in my head. It's almost like taking a piece of God with you.

I do listen to music that is both inspirational and that I can sing to, because it's my way of expressing my emotions in a way that's all mine, and I'm sharing it with myself. Music has always been very powerful for me. It connects me in a way to my soul. I feel very deeply through music. I find it's one of the wonderful gifts of life—corny, but very true.
—ROSE MARY AQUAVIA

It wasn't until I started to attend synagogue services with my wife that I started to feel some sort of connection to my spiritual side. This was in no small part due to the music, despite the fact that it was in Hebrew and I understood only the odd word. The depth of emotion emanating from the music as sung by the cantor and choir is so strong that words aren't necessary to convey what I need to hear. After going to Mass every Sunday as a child, the words of the hymns had lost their meaning for me. I was just responding to what the priest said and not really understanding why we were saying these things.

Hashkiveinu *is sung with such conviction that knowing the words might actually ruin it for me.* Adon Olam *(which our congregation sings to a Sephardic melody) is such a triumphant song that one can't help being inspired and finding a connection that has been missing for far too long.*

Finding your spiritual side isn't something that can be forced upon you; each of us must find it for ourselves. Sometimes it just sneaks up on you from an unexpected source. I was attending these services out of love and respect for my wife and her beliefs, and I found out something about myself in the process.

—JOHN O'HARE

I was selected for a jury on a case of murder involving a teenage victim and defendant. The trial was filled with horrible exhibits and sordid testimony about drug use, teen pregnancy and convoluted, unhappy family relationships. As I left the courthouse each day, completely exhausted, my head was filled with ugly pictures.

Driving home after a day in court, I'd turn on the car radio to one of the classical music stations. I have never been more thankful for the beauty of Mozart, Brahms and other composers. By the time I arrived home, I felt as if I had taken a spiritual shower. The music wiped away the ugliness and filled my soul with peace.

—BARBARA ABORN

Be a Nature Lover

BEING AROUND NATURE is one of the most elemental ways of getting in touch with God. Even if you don't necessarily believe that a huge, mystical Creator brought the world into being in six days just by willing it so or that every blade of grass that grows is there for a great cosmic reason, it's impossible to observe the natural world and not feel at least some sense of awe at the marvelous way it works. There is an order, power, beauty and mystery that we may never be able to comprehend in its entirety.

But the longing to be around it is a basic human need. Even in the midst of our concrete and glass cities, we make room for potted trees and window boxes. We live in a culture of comfort unparalleled in any generation before us, and yet we spend our weekends hiking in parks and our vacations camping out. We challenge ourselves by climbing up steep cliffs, rafting through churning whitecapped rivers and biking through rocky terrain, not so much for the exercise as for the opportunity to confront the natural forces that will never be entirely tamed by humankind.

For three days this week, go out and find ways to appreciate nature. You can start with the simple things. Watch the sun rise or set. Find a flower and admire its color, its petals, its scent. Walk through a wooded park. Go to the beach and sit watching the waves, thinking about the millions of years of tides coming in and out. Look at a bee collecting pollen or a colony of ants swarming around its hill.

If you're up for it, try activities that put you right in the middle of the outdoors. Take an introductory rafting, skiing or rock-climbing class. Find a comfortable hiking or biking trail. Learn astronomy and watch the constellations change. Camp out in your backyard.

Don't forget the weather. Instead of running for shelter or taking out your umbrella when the rain comes, stand outside and feel it on your face. Play in the snow instead of rushing to shovel it. On a fiercely hot day (like the one most of the country suffered through in the summer of 1999), sit outside—just for a few minutes, not long enough to pass out. Meditate on the power of the sun and remember what a vital part it plays in the lives of all living things. (Okay, now you can duck back into your air-conditioned living room.) Even if, like me, you're terrified of thunderstorms, try to watch one at least once (indoors, please). Lightning is as magnificent as it is dangerous.

Don't let the changes of the seasons pass you by. Pick a tree you see every day and try to catch the precise moment the leaf buds start to open in the spring. A few months later, observe the leaves turning without worrying about having to rake them all. Smell the sharpness of cold air and the softness of warm breezes.

As often as you can, visit places where nature takes precedence over civilization: thick forests, unspoiled beaches, mountains, canyons, lakes, prairies, deserts. Think about the millions of years these places have existed and the millions more they will see long after our grandchildren's grandchildren are gone. The more you come to appreciate these gifts of the earth, the more likely you'll be to want to preserve them from man-made ravages.

In the next chapter, we'll look at an even simpler way to commune with nature on a daily basis.

The way I spend time in nature varies widely. Some weeks, it's an all-out activity like a hike in the woods or a swim in a lake; more often, it's snatches of time on my lunch hour, where I go out on a dock near my office in Jersey City and look into the water. I'm usually drawn to water and trees when I decide to spend time outdoors. The more time I spend, the more I feel "healed," as if I've just done something nurturing for myself. I always feel more in touch with God when I look at the amazing things in nature. Being outdoors feels like therapeutic time.
—LYNN COWAN

When I was in college, I remember sitting on the bleachers on a cold, clear night watching a friend's soccer game. Looking up at the moon and stars made me remember what I had learned in science class that week, about the Big Bang theory and how the planets were formed and how earth came to be.

Just looking up there and thinking of my place in it all made me a little dizzy and awed, and though I felt very small, I also felt special.
—VALERIE KALFRIN

Back to the Garden

WHEN I WAS about fourteen, I was fascinated with the idea of growing my own avocado plant—I'm not sure why now, since I don't think I liked avocados much then. But I bought a book on the subject and, with a little help from Mom, I prepared a pit by stabbing it with toothpicks and suspending it over a glass of water filled high enough to reach the bottom.

It seemed to take forever, but just as the book promised, the pit eventually cracked and sprouted little roots. Suddenly, it wasn't just a piece of trash, but a foundation for life. When the roots were well established, I carefully planted the pit into a flowerpot and cheered when a thin trunk broke through the soil a couple of weeks later. From then on, there was no stopping it. The trunk became taller. Notches became branches. Branches formed buds. Buds turned into leaves.

The book warned me not to expect a rich harvest anytime soon—apparently, avocados are sensitive and rather lazy, requiring cross-pollination to rouse them into producing fruit. Without a swarm of cooperative bees to help out, my plant was doomed to a perpetual state of birth control. But I wasn't in this for the guacamole. What excited me was that, with just a little effort and care, I had taken a plain seed and coaxed it into becoming something more. Nature had taken its course, but I was the one who had given it a jump-start. I felt satisfied, proud—and maybe just a bit powerful.

A year or two later, I experimented in the garden, planting zinnias, string beans and peas. The flowers only lasted a couple of seasons, but it was still thrilling to see their pink, purple and orange heads bobbing a greeting when I passed by every day. And the vegetable plants never amounted to much—a few fistfuls, barely enough for dinner—but I couldn't have been happier with my meager harvest if it had been a dozen bushels.

I might not have told you back then that gardening was my way of communing with God, but on some level, I think I knew that working with these plants made me feel more spiritual.

I suspect that's one of the reasons so many of us keep gardens, even in the smallest spaces (in my neighborhood, people crowd beautiful riots of flowers into front yards barely five feet square). We hang spider plants in baskets on the wall, display petunias and geraniums in window boxes and bring out pots of amaryllis, poinsettia and paperwhites in the winter. While there's no question that the colors and arrangements are aesthetically pleasing, the satisfaction we get from them goes much deeper than that. When we coax a zucchini from a tiny seed or a rosebush from a spiky ball of dirt, we're experiencing a mystery that almost defies definition. An unseen force is guiding these little potentialities to life and light, and we can't control it. All we can do is provide the right conditions: the proper soil; water enough to quench without drowning; a few extra vitamins; substances to ward off hungry insects.

Caring for a plot of plants also brings us out into the blessing of other natural wonders that thrill the senses: the warm sun on our neck; the rich loamy smell of soil and the crumbling of clods between our fingers; the ants, worms and potato bugs that carry on their business, barely acknowledging our existence; birds singing on branches nearby; the grass—and, yes, weeds—that come back without any effort on our part. No wonder the poem says: "One is nearer to God in a garden/Than anyplace else on earth."

Gardening is a wonderful form of meditation, too; it provides just the right combination of mindfulness and mental freedom needed to bring ourselves into a sense of peace. It's hard to obsess about a work-related problem when you're cutting an arrangement of roses or pulling out a stubborn dandelion.

Your exercise now is to find time to care for a plant at least once a week. If you already have a garden, you're ahead of the game. Go out there and put your heart into it. Focus on the smells of the flowers and earth. Listen to your spade ringing and your heart beating. Be aware of the season, whether you're watching the first crocuses peek through or wrapping your tomato plants up for the winter. Feel the satisfaction of getting the plot in order.

If you don't have a garden, try to put even a little something in your yard. You don't have to be Martha Stewart on the first go; just dig out a corner and plant something that appeals to you—daffodils, broccoli, a box-wood bush. Ask a nursery expert how to care for your new addition and watch it become a part of your surroundings. You might wonder how you ever lived without it.

And if you live in an apartment or aren't physically able to put the time into a full-fledged garden, there are still ways to meet your floral needs. Start an herb garden in your kitchen—they're easy to care for, and you'll have fresh basil for your spaghetti sauce, to boot. Hang a basket. Grow some grass for your cat to nibble. Buy a little potted plant or a bonsai tree. Get a Chia Pet. Whatever works for you. (You can fill vases with cut flowers, too, but it's not the same thing. Get something that will grow while you watch.)

Be aware of the lessons you learn as you go. Remember my avocado plant? Well, the story's not done yet. According to the book I bought, avocados have to be cut back every so often to allow the plant to sprout and flourish. Yet I couldn't bring myself to do it—how could I be sure that cutting off the top branches would make it look any better? What if I ruined it forever?

So I continued to water, care and talk to it (people

conversed with their plants a lot back then), but despite my ministrations, the avocado stayed thin and spindly. It stopped producing new branches. One by one, the leaves turned yellow, curled and dropped off. Less than a year after the pit sprouted, the plant was beyond rescue. I put it in the trash, knowing now that to flourish, plants have to be guided, even if it hurts a little. Once I passed adolescence, I learned that the same holds true of people.

Then there are times when no guidance is necessary. My parents had a camellia bush on their front lawn that produced beautiful magenta flowers and dark, glossy leaves without fail every year. Then came one winter—an unusually cold one for our area—that froze everything in its path. The camellia bush turned brown; when spring came, there were no buds. The delicate flowers were no match for the freeze. But it was a big bush that would have required strong professional workers to unearth (no cheap task), and my parents never got around to hiring anyone.

So the withered bush stayed, and one year became two became fifteen. Then one spring day, my mother was coming into the house when she was startled by something she hadn't seen in ages—a single camellia blossom peeking out. But she chalked it up as an oddity and figured it was the bush's very last, long-delayed gasp.

The next year, the blossom was back—and this time, it had brought a friend. And the bush continued to recover. The leaves regained their dark sheen. More and more flowers appeared every spring. Today, it's as beautiful as it was on the day we moved into the house. To look at it, you'd never know it had been through such an ordeal.

Did God deliberately resurrect the bush as a lesson in time, patience and renewal? Perhaps not. But I like to think that we serve God when we learn from working with plants.

I bought a house about a year ago and have begun gardening. I find pulling up weeds and tending to flowers, fruits and vegetables to be very spiritual. I can get lost in the rhythm of the work. I feel like I am giving back to the earth in some way. It clears my head and allows me to focus on nothing else but what I can do for the plants. The thought and feeling of these living things needing me is in a way fulfilling and overwhelming—in a good way.
—ROSE MARY AQUAVIA

Animal Instincts

As I WRITE THIS, Smokey is curled up on the bed, dreaming whatever little furry dreams go through the mind of a pampered gray cat. Just a few minutes ago, he was leaping and swatting at his favorite feather fishing toy, every nerve in his body centered on the task at hand. Later, he might decide to perch on the sill to watch the children playing outside. I wonder if he has any idea how wise he is?

The comic strip *Rose Is Rose* has a cat named Peekaboo who fancies himself a guru, and I don't think the cartoonist means this to be a joke. Animals, when you think about it, are very spiritual creatures. They've mastered the art of living in the moment without being aware of it. They don't wake up worrying about something that happened last week, and when they go to sleep at night, they've completely forgotten about any little wrongs that may have happened during the day. When they set out to do something—be it eating or grooming or getting to know the cocker spaniel next door—they focus their full attention on the activity. A cat scratching at her post isn't thinking about the letter she owes her friend. When you play fetch with your dog, he's not sighing to himself because he really ought to be checking out the trees instead. Animals listen to their bodies. They eat when their stomachs tell them to. They exercise and stretch their muscles. (When a pet is lazy, it's usually because we're not giving them the activity time it needs.) When they relax, they rest their entire bodies. And they don't need a steady stream of noise or televised entertainment to keep them from getting bored.

They appreciate and seek out pleasure as a part of their everyday activity, rather than taking it sparingly and only after the chores are done. It doesn't matter if the dishes aren't washed—if there's a warm sunbeam on the floor, it's time to lie down and bask in it. Most animals play from the time they can stand on their own; yes, they're learning survival skills as they go, but it's fun, too. Some animals invent games for themselves for no particular reason. My husband once saw a dolphin take a fish his trainer had fed him and toss it to one side of his pen, which opened out into the ocean. When a school of fish started swimming toward the bait, the dolphin swam over, grabbed the food and tossed it to the other side of the pen, playing a "keep-away" of sorts with the puzzled fish. One recent study even showed that rats love to be tickled—and giggle when their stomachs are scratched!

Then, of course, there's the whole issue of unconditional love. A pet doesn't decide to be your best friend one day and then change his mind because he's found a better companion. They don't think any less of you because you didn't get the promotion or because you paid a bill late or because you're a Braves fan. Just the very fact that you're sharing your life with them is good enough. In most cases, you really have to go a long way to make a dog or cat mistrust you, and there are any number of stories of abused and neglected pets who still found it in their hearts to love a more caring owner.

If you have an animal or know someone who does, spend a few hours with it and see what it teaches you about spirituality. Even a fish or a snake has a lesson for us about grace, silence and awareness. Go to a zoo and check out wildlife from elephants to alligators to tiny lemurs, all content with their own existence and utterly unconcerned about what tomorrow holds. If that's not spiritual, I don't know what is.

The way animals treat each other is worth noting, too. It may be disturbing to see a lion pouncing on a sick zebra or wolves fighting over territory, but the things they do are strictly motivated by self-preservation. There's no concept in their minds of hatred or vindictiveness or grudge-holding. A lion who's just eaten a full meal doesn't turn around and attack a gazelle because it's bored or frustrated or doesn't like the way its antlers look. Think, too, of the examples we hear of animals who look out for each other, sometimes at the risk of their own lives. Whales will beach themselves in the effort to guide back a member of the pod who has drifted too close to shore. Meerkats "babysit" the young of their group and watch for signs of danger while hunters go off in search of food for everyone. Think of Binti-Jua, the zoo gorilla who rescued a young boy who had tumbled into the ape enclosure and brought him to the keepers' door. Or Scarlett, the brave cat who plunged into a fiery building not once but five times to save her kittens, despite the terrible pain she must have been suffering. Should not we, whose intellect and reason are far superior to that of any other earthly being, feel a responsibility to act at least as decently as that—and more, to resist the urge that drives us to hate and to hurt?

When Smokey sits in my lap, his bright green eyes half-closing, it's really quite a miracle when you think about it. Here I am, this being so much bigger than he is, whose language he doesn't speak and whose commands often don't make sense to him. Occasionally I do things that startle or frighten him, and I don't always let him have his way. But he never fails to trust me, huge and mysterious as I am. He seeks me out, showers me with affection and rumbles an appreciative purr for the kindnesses I show.

If we were only half as trusting and loving toward God, we'd be way ahead of the game.

Whenever I've had a stressful day, picking up one of my many animals and letting it either sit on my shoulder (if it's one of my chinchillas or gerbils), or fall asleep in my lap (if it's my dog) is the greatest reason to come home I can think of. Nothing else comforts me like my animals. If I'm sad or depressed, I just crawl on the couch, and my dog curls up next to me. We usually nap, and when I wake up, whatever was causing me grief just doesn't seem as important. I know that God loves animals, and I absolutely believe that when my pets are gone, we will all walk into Heaven together. Having my animals trust me, and enjoy being petted (especially the rodents, who are notorious for hating any sort of restraint!), is one of the reasons I got into veterinary medicine and every day I am so grateful to have this career ahead of me.

—JODI HOLCOMB

As you wrap up your week, take a minute to answer these questions:

What did I like most about this week?

What did I like least?

Did these exercises make me feel calmer? Less stressed?

Have these exercises helped me with other aspects of my daily life?   If so, which?

Do I feel closer to God now?   If so, how?

What was the most interesting thing I learned this week?

What do I want to work on in the coming week?

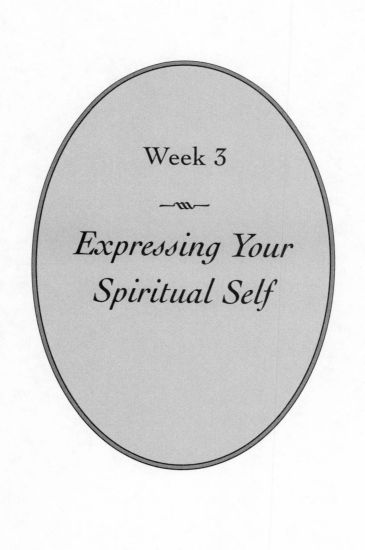

Week 3

Expressing Your
Spiritual Self

Now that you know more about what makes you feel spiritual, you're going to show that knowledge off this week through creative exercises. When you read the next few chapters, they may strike you as a little odd. Painting? Singing? Arranging objects on a table? *Sex?!* What does that have to do with God?

Everything, that's what. Remember, God isn't some limited entity that can only be accessed at certain hours of the day or in a particular place. We can feel and find God anytime we like and in any manner that reaches the most genuine and devout part of ourselves. Put it this way: Is the ceiling of the Sistine Chapel merely a piece of commissioned artwork, devoid of any soul? Do Tibetan monks spend months making elaborate mandala patterns out of colored sand simply because they don't have access to paint-by-numbers kits? And—don't blush now—after a particularly beautiful and intimate lovemaking session, haven't you felt . . . well, blessed?

The exercises this week only begin to touch on the many creative ways in which you can take joy in your spirit. I hope that they inspire you to find others. And when you do, I hope you'll let me know!

Finding Your Inner Artist

REMEMBER WHEN absolute bliss meant smearing finger-prints around a big piece of paper for an hour? When you squished modeling clay between your fingers, trying to get the shape just right? When you had the power to turn macaroni, glitter and fabric into works of art just by applying your imagination and a few generous smears of Elmer's glue?

You were being spiritual without even knowing it. Creating art of any kind is an act that involves the part of our souls we usually don't tap into on a daily basis. We rely on our emotions, our intuition and our heart to lead us to the finished product. We use art to express our innermost selves, to bring us closer to our sense of the divine.

The trouble is, many of us haven't done anything creative since we cut out paper snowflakes in third grade. "I was never any good at it," we say. Or "My stuff will never hang on a museum wall, so what's the point?" It's so easy to neglect the artist in us because most of day-to-day living is so uncreative. We don't need art to raise the kids or attend a meeting or pay the bills, so we assume that it's nonessential for all but the few people lucky enough to be able to make a living at it.

Wrong, wrong, wrong. If anything, we need to express ourselves through art more now as adults than we did as children. For one thing, it's a terrific release for stress—when you're totally engrossed in capturing a still life or shaping a clay bowl, the rest of the world automatically shuts itself out.

We need the outlet for our emotions, too. Think of the last time you felt overwhelming joy and didn't know of any other way to share it but to wear a silly grin all day. Or the frustration that led you to reach for a pint of Ben & Jerry's or head to the mall to buy something you didn't really need. There was the anger that made you shout out nasty insults you regretted later. Or the times you've felt miserable for no particular reason. Wouldn't it be better to put some of that misery on paper rather than moping around? Some of the greatest works of art in the world were created by men and women in the heights of ecstasy and the depths of despair.

So this week, pick at least one day to become an artist. To start, find a medium that suits you. Crafts stores have basic pastel, charcoal, watercolor and paint sets. Borrow your kids' jumbo box of crayons. Raid your pantry for macaroni and glue. Or just pick up a pencil and paper—whatever seems to be calling out to you. My mother used to make imaginative creations out of seashells, rocks, sharks' teeth and metallic spray paint. My dad recently started putting together collages out of pictures clipped from magazines—he'll work on one for hours. I have one of his works at home now, a stunning group of images representing the creation of the earth. But you don't have to stick to biblical themes or any themes at all, for that matter. Just get the pencil or brush to the paper and see what comes to mind. Paint the color of trees after rain. Draw an emotion. Ask your heart what it wants to create.

The messier arts—clay, finger paints and the like—are a great choice for freeing the mind and spirit. There's something about getting your hands nice and dirty that can be very liberating. Just spread out a lot of newspaper, put on an old T-shirt to wipe your fingers with and let yourself go. Slosh, slop, squish all you want. Feel your hands smearing and slipping. Marvel at how the colors mix or how many textures you can create on a glob of Play-Doh.

The one thing I advise against is working from a kit or one of those TV programs that show you how to paint a particular object or scene. That's not being spiritually creative; that's just following someone else's idea of what a still life or ocean should look like. (Go to any garage sale, and you'll see at least one homemade painting that was obviously an attempt to copy something out of a book or a Bob Ross lesson.) And no fair using clip-and-paste art on your computer. This is your personal creation. Use your own work, your own imagination.

Whatever you do, be gentle with yourself. Don't rip up your work because a line didn't come out right or the paint dripped in the wrong place. We've all heard the little voice of the self-censor inside our head—the one that makes gagging noises and says, *That looks terrible! Who said you could do anything creative? Better pack it in and go back to doing the laundry.* Before you even begin, turn off that censor and plunge ahead, no matter what the result. If a line comes out wrong, erase it and start again. If the paint dribbles, work with it. If the pot is lopsided, so what? Nobody ever said, "The *Venus de Milo* would be so much more beautiful if it had arms."

Give yourself permission not to be perfect when you're creating artwork. Come to think of it, that's a spiritual lesson in itself. God doesn't ask us to do everything perfectly—only to put a perfect heart into what we do. The point isn't to make a masterpiece worthy of hanging in the Louvre. It doesn't even have to be good enough to stick onto your refrigerator. It just has to come from your heart. If you come away feeling satisfied that you've expressed yourself, you've done it right.

My earliest effort at fabricating a collage was based on the idea of depicting the creation of the universe in accordance with the now-popular scientific theory nicknamed "the big bang." At the outset, things went poorly, both artistically and intellectually. Then I was suddenly struck with the thought of merging the scientific and the biblical versions of Creation into one integrated representation.

At first, the thought of merging the two seemed strange to me. It somehow suggested the use of science to prove the existence of God—something I have always been skeptical of. But I soon realized that placing God in juxtaposition with science had nothing to do with "proof," scientific or otherwise. I forged ahead and put a Michelangelo-like portrayal of God at the very top, and showed Him hurling the primeval atom into empty space, which then explodes and expands into a brightly colored array of galaxies, nebulae, stars and, further down, living organisms. The collage is titled The Big Bang. *It could just as appropriately be titled* God Said, "Let There Be Light." *I am happy with it either way.*

—MURRAY ABORN

Your Personal Altar

THE TOP of my computer desk is overflowing with photographs. There's me in my graduation gown with my parents on either side. My brother, holding a small bird of prey. The college friends, still among my closest pals after all these years—one smiling in her senior picture, one in her karate *gi*, another coaxing a reluctant cat to pose for the camera. And shots from no fewer than half a dozen weddings.

Filling in the gaps between the pictures are silly little plastic figurines: Warner Bros. cartoon characters, a bear in a nun's habit, a "computer goddess" meant to ward off viruses and keep the hard drive from crashing.

When I first arranged the mementos on the shelf, I thought I was just livening up an otherwise ordinary piece of furniture. Only later did I realize I had created a shrine.

Shrines and altars aren't just for houses of worship, and they don't necessarily have to be decorated with religious icons. If you have a family portrait on the piano, that's a shrine. So is the collection of souvenirs from the summer you spent abroad. There are shrines in office cubicles, bedrooms and gardens. There are shrines as elaborate as any cathedral and as simple as a seashell. And no two are exactly identical.

What really defines a shrine is the meaning you give to the objects in it. The pictures on my desk are a constant reminder of the important people in my life and the special times we've shared. They're happy moments, frozen in time and ready to give me a boost after a hard day. I see the wedding pictures and feel inspired that all these friends have managed to keep their marriages strong after so many years. And though the cartoon toys might seem silly to anyone else, they actually connect me to my husband, John, with whom I've laughed a thousand times over Bugs Bunny and Pinky and the Brain. He also studies animation, so the figures are a reminder of a dream that may yet come true one day. Finally, they *are* silly—and a lesson to me not to take life so seriously.

SOMETIMES shrines are a means of keeping alive the memory of a dear one. Several years ago, Barbara Taylor's youngest daughter, Krissy, a vivacious young woman with a promising modeling career, died suddenly at home at the far-too-young age of seventeen. (Tests later showed that an undiagnosed heart condition was the cause.) Needing more than just a gravesite to honor their beloved child, Barbara and her husband received permission from a park near their home in Florida to plant a royal poinciana tree in a quiet spot. In a memorial service, the parents and Krissy's two older sisters Joie and Niki planted sunflower seeds—Krissy's favorite flower—around the trunk and set a stone with her name in the earth nearby. Friends and family read letters and poems, played the country music Krissy loved, then set off fireworks in the night sky.

The Taylors visit the tree often, separately and together. Sometimes they hang mementos from the branches, such as homemade mobiles or wind chimes; sometimes they do some light weeding and landscaping around the site; sometimes they just sit quietly, reflecting on their memories. To them, the tree is a living tribute to a beautiful young woman, and it brings Krissy closer to them in ways nothing else can.

Barbara believes her daughter's spirit is very much present in this spot. The poinciana, which blooms only once a year, always seems to put forth its bright orange-red blossoms right around Mother's Day. Last year, she noticed that four little trees had sprouted around the trunk—though no one had transplanted any new greenery there. "Krissy always wanted to be a mother," Barbara says. "Those are the children she never had."

Now it's your turn to work on your own shrine. Chances are you've got one already. Set aside a space that appeals to you, one that you're sure to see at least once a day. A tabletop or windowsill will do, though you can make yours bigger if you like. Then fill it with objects that make you want to meditate or smile or cry or think or pray. You can use as many as you like, but be sure not to pile on so many that you can't see any one item easily.

Be careful, too, not to confuse a shrine with a collection. It's fun to amass salt and pepper shakers or Beanie Babies or Tiffany glass, but more often than not, the point is to collect as many and as wide or rare a variety as possible, not selecting only the ones that resonate deep in your soul. Sure, you might use a teacup from your collection in your shrine because your grandmother gave it to you or the stuffed Eeyore doll because it reminds you of your husband when he first wakes up in the morning, but don't put the entire set of cups or dolls on your altar unless all of them really have special significance for you.

Once you have your shrine arranged the way you like it, take at least five minutes every day to sit before it and meditate on all or part of it. Let the memories and emotions come as they will. Reflect on what the items say about you as a person and about your life.

Try rearranging your shrine once a month or whenever the mood hits you. Add something new and see what happens. Put away a couple of objects; allow yourself to miss them, then see what the shrine offers without them. When you celebrate holidays or go on vacation, keep your eyes open for possible additions.

Above all, your shrine should bring you peace. And when it does, remember the feeling, so you'll know the sensation when it comes along at other times of the day.

Sing It!

NOW THAT YOU'VE LEARNED how to listen to music prayer-fully, it's time for you to make some of your own.

Just as drawing or painting can express your inner-most spiritual feelings, singing can help you connect to God in a way that prayer sometimes can't. Think of Muslims and Hindus chanting as they worship. Think of gospel groups and the Mormon Tabernacle Choir. Think of cantors in synagogues, whose main purpose is to sing certain prayers and lead the congregation in song.

To give you a better idea of how important it is to use singing to express spirituality, I'll share some of my bat mitzvah speech with you. (You knew I had to fit this in somewhere.) I chose the *Shirat Ha'Yam* ("Song of the Sea") as my Torah portion, precisely because it brings up such wonderful meditations about the role of song in wor-ship. This section is the point in Exodus just after Moses and the children of Israel have crossed the Sea of Reeds safely and seen their Egyptian foes perish as the water spilled back onto them.

You'd think that the Hebrews would have had lots to do after that. They were probably in need of food, water, a bath, a place to rest for the night. They should have been counting heads, discussing what had just happened, maybe crying tears of joy and relief. But no, the first thing they did, as soon as the crisis had passed, was sing, praising God for the gift of freedom and marveling at the great Power that had brought the proud, tyrannical enemy down. "Give thanks to God, for He is very great!" the song goes. "The horse and his rider He has cast into the sea."

Not only that, but the women—led by Moses' sister, Miriam—were dancing and shaking their tambourines as they sang. Who thinks to pack a musical instrument when you're running away from slavery? Better to leave it behind and pack something practical, like an extra water bag or a sack of grain. But they were so confident that God would triumph—and so sure that they would be singing afterward—that they made room for their timbrels in their carts.

Still more interesting is the fact that this is the first example of song in the Bible. Nobody sings when the world is created, when the great Flood subsides or when Joseph reunites with his family. But when Israel is redeemed and the journey to become a nation begins, the Israelites burst into song because they can do no less. The joy in their hearts is too great, their gratitude too inexpressible, their awe too overwhelming. The passage begins: "Then Moses and the children of Israel sang this song . . ." and sages have debated the importance of that first word. Perhaps only after they sang could the liberation be considered a miracle.

So if these newly freed people could express their thanks to God in song, why shouldn't we?

Make an effort at least once this week to let your musical voice be heard. The easiest way, of course, is to attend a religious service and join in the hymns. Don't worry about being heard by the people around you. They're more concerned about themselves. Just let your song ring out.

Depending on what time of year you're reading this, you could also find a public event at which you can join in singing Christmas carols, Chanukah songs or the Easter Sunday rendition of Handel's *Hallelujah Chorus*. Even if you're so familiar with the words and melodies that you could recite them in your sleep, approach them with a new eye. Pretend you're performing for an audience of One. How would you phrase the lyrics? What meaning would you give them? How much energy would you put into the song? You might never sing *Adeste Fidelis* the same way again.

If you'd rather not go public just yet, then do your singing at home. Sing to your children. Sing as you do the dishes, make the bed or vacuum. Sing in that ever-popular music hall, the shower, and listen to your voice echo off the walls. You can use songs you already know or make up some of your own, using messages you want to express at that given moment (*God is with me; peace to us all; I am connected to the earth; give praise for this day; Spirit is everywhere; my Sabbath has come; Amen!*). Or take a psalm and invent your own tune.

Don't worry about the way you sound. This isn't about musical talent; it's about expressing yourself. Too often, we stifle our voices for fear of being criticized by others—and I'm not just talking about singing. When we withhold the right to express ourselves, we lose something bigger and more precious in the process: the ability to share our unique, powerful thoughts with the world and with God.

So forget about pitch and tone. Go for the emotion and the personal meaning. This is your time and your voice. Make yourself heard. Let God know you're there.

When you become more comfortable with impromptu singing, experiment a little. Buy CDs or tapes of sacred music that's new to you—Gregorian chants, Hindi songs, Native American dances, earth-shaking gospel—and sing along.

As the quote goes: "Make a joyful noise unto the Lord." Why deny God something that's so much fun to do?

Blessings

ONE OF THE AMAZING THINGS about spirituality is the ability to transform things at will. With a few simple words, we change plain grape juice into consecrated wine. An ordinary meal becomes something extraordinary. A stick becomes an instrument through which a group decrees who will next speak his turn. Objects we take for granted at other times become symbols of peace or courageous deeds or great sacrifices.

Blessings are powerful things. They transform, protect, empower, reassure. When we give our blessings, we actually join forces with God, the Source of the actual blessing, and reaffirm our faith that good things will happen if we only wait and trust.

Since it takes very little time or effort to give a blessing, do it at least four times this week. Here are some ideas to get you started:

· Take at least one meal and say a blessing over it. You can use either a standard familiar prayer or try creating one of your own. The important thing is to make it meaningful to you, whether you're expressing gratitude for all that you have or wonder at the goodness of the foods you eat. Then notice how much more special the meal is once it has been blessed. Take your time eating; concentrate on the flavors, textures and juices. Continue the sense of gratitude throughout the meal.

· Bless your children before they leave for school. Imagine your words joining with God's power to form a protective field around them as they study and play.

· Bless someone who sneezes and put some feeling into it. Imagine that your blessing is actually keeping this person from serious illness. If the sneezes keep coming, put more energy into your blessing.

· Bless someone who is ill, sending healing thoughts as you say it.

· Bless your home whenever you go out—even if you just murmur a quick, "Bless this house." Feel an unseen Presence standing guard, watching when you can't.

· Say a short blessing before having sex. Ask that it be both a passionate and spiritual experience.

· If you belong to a spirituality circle (and if not, you'll learn how later in this book), be sure to offer blessings on the group before each meeting.

· At work, give a silent blessing before important meetings

or lectures. Ask God to bring your officemates together as a team and to let the creative energy flow.

· In your garden, bless everything around you—from the soil to the plants, the trees, insects, birds, your tools, the rain. Imagine God's hand helping all these elements work together harmoniously to produce shelter, fruit, pollen, color and life.

· Bless every object on your personal altars as you create them and every new item you add to them after that. Ask that they always be a source of inspiration.

· Think of blessings for all the work you do—your artwork, your cooking, your job assignments, your kisses.

ONCE YOU'VE GOTTEN into the habit, make a note of it in your journal. How do your personal blessings affect your life? Do you feel any kind of partnership with God? Do you feel more protected or protecting? Do the people you bless seem happier, calmer, more grateful? Are there certain blessings that seem more effective than others? Has anyone blessed you lately?

As always, keep going with what works and continue to experiment. Say a blessing for people you don't even know—from the children left homeless by war and earthquakes to world leaders gathered to make decisions that will affect millions.

Oh yes, one more thing—bless you for giving this exercise a try.

Spiritual Sex

IT MAY SEEM out of place to include a chapter on sex in a book about spirituality. It's such a basic, earthy, primal act—how could it possibly relate to the effort to become closer to a Higher Power?

And yet, done in the proper frame of mind, sex can be an intensely spiritual act. It's not as though lovemaking never appears in the Bible—if you leaf through it, you'll see references to "lying down with" and "knowing" women. But those passages are very matter-of-fact, almost mechanical. They're simple cause and effect: The wives and concubines lie down with men, then go on to "begat" generation after generation.

But spiritual love appears there, too. Read the Song of Solomon (Song of Songs). It's a magnificent piece of poetry, but it's also some of the most impassioned sentiment you'll ever read. The two lovers yearn for each other, compare each other's bodies to young, vibrant animals, the sweetest fruits and new wine. They sing:

> Let me be a seal upon your heart,
>> Like the seal upon your hand.
> For love is fierce as death,
>> Passion is mighty as Sheol.
> Its darts are darts of fire,
>> A blazing flame.
> Vast floods cannot quench love,
>> Nor rivers drown it.
> If a man offered all his wealth for love,
>> He would be laughed to scorn.

Far from being a shameful or secret desire, the passion of love can be a marvelous, even transcendent experience.

But we don't always treat it that way. We have sex out of loneliness and spite, out of pity and desperation. We choose the wrong partners. We choose the right ones for the wrong reasons. We make it a chore or a rote routine. We deny ourselves pleasure. We don't ask for what we want. We rush to finish or become reluctant to begin. We confuse quantity with quality. We don't take the time to really appreciate our partners. We don't bring our Higher Power into the act. And so we walk away unsatisfied, restless, wanting more or not wanting enough. We write it off as just another part of the relationship to be dealt with. We make excuses. We let our sex life slide. Sometimes we stop making love entirely for days, weeks, months, years, decades.

But the key to making love spiritually—like the key to doing so many other things spiritually—is to be fully present in the moment. We have a tendency to leave our minds elsewhere when we go about our daily routines, and love-making is no exception. We worry: *Do I look too fat?* and *Do we have time for this before going to work?* We think: *Boy, am I tired right now,* and *When is he going to finish?* In the middle of foreplay, we mentally jump ahead to the next step; in the middle of sex, our minds turn to what we'll be doing after we're done. Sometimes, we even bring another partner into the mix by fantasizing. That's not to say that fantasies are a bad thing in themselves or even that they can't make a sex life fun and invigorating. But for spiritual sex, fantasies are unwelcome because they bring another person into the bedroom. When you're thinking about being ravaged by Mel Gibson or Cindy Crawford, you're not being fully in the moment, and you're not participating actively with your partner. You've got your mind on an imaginary scenario, hoping to get better results than you've come to expect from being with the person you love.

This next exercise, should you choose to accept it, will help open your awareness of lovemaking as a spiritual act. I suggest this primarily for married couples or long-term partners, since they presumably have a greater knowledge of each other and a willingness to be vulnerable in front of each other, which are vital ingredients here. But if you have a partner with whom you feel you can share this kind of intimacy, by all means try it.

Here's how you allow spirituality into the bedroom:

First, choose an hour of the night (or day) in which you can take all the time you need. Yes, quickies can be spiritual, too, but for starters, you don't want to feel the constraints of time. This time is to be uninterrupted. Unplug the phone, lock the door and make sure the kids know you're not available unless someone is bleeding from the ears.

Set an atmosphere that's comfortable for both of you. Light candles or oil lamps, play music (very softly) in the background, scent the room with incense, perfume or oil. If you have a set of sheets you particularly like, make the bed with them ahead of time. What you wear isn't as important as how comfortable you feel in it. If you feel more fully yourself in flannel pajamas rather than a camisole and garter belt, wear the pajamas. Or start off wearing nothing at all. Surround yourself with sensuality.

You and your partner should start off by sitting next to each other, looking into each other's eyes. They say the eyes are the windows to the soul—what do you see in his? In hers? Don't try to guess what your partner is thinking. Just sit there and accept him or her as he or she is.

Try the Tantric technique of breathing together. Take deep, slow breaths in through the nose and out through the mouth, in sync. Imagine that you are giving life to each other or that by inhaling and exhaling in unison, you both are one with each other and with the universe.

Then slowly, begin to touch each other. Don't start with the genitals; instead, focus on less obvious areas (the face, the ears, the shoulders, the knees). Take your time. Experiment with light, sweeping touches and deep-but-gentle rubbing. You might even want to give each other a mutual back, foot or head rub before beginning, to relax you and put you in the mood.

Above all, as you go, keep your senses aware of what you do. Feel the softness of skin and the coarseness of hair, the sensations that come from being touched by fingers, palms and lips. Smell the perfume, shampoo, soap and linen. Hear your breathing, gentle and deep. When you kiss, be aware of tastes. Keep your eyes open, if you can, and watch what your lover does to you. Look at your lover's body and turn whatever criticisms you might have into assets. For instance, you might think of that extra padding around the stomach and thighs as beautiful, sensuous flesh to touch. A wrinkle or a spider vein is just a mark etched by laughter or experience. Think of your partner as perfect in the eyes of God, and then it will be easier to think of him or her as perfect in your eyes, too.

In the Eastern tradition, coming to orgasm is only a part of the entire experience, not the central point of it, and that happens only after a prolonged period (some couples delay for hours or days). That might be a bit much to shoot for right now, but in that spirit, you'll want to hold off from genital caressing or contact until both of you are thoroughly excited and fully ready for the actual intercourse. Then have fun. Experiment with positions or speeds or intensity. Try stopping just before the point of no return, rest for a couple of minutes and then picking up where you left off.

Don't shut yourself off to the final moments of pleasure. Don't hold back. Move or make noise as the urge takes you. Enjoy yourself and consider yourself lucky to be human and able to take such delight in such a basic act.

Afterward, don't shut each other out. Kiss or cuddle for a few minutes. Keep the warmth and affection going before resuming your lives. Revel in the pleasure you can give and receive. You might even say a quick prayer of thanks for the perfection of your bodies, the gift of each other and the mystery of sex that only God knows completely.

Time to sum up Week 3—your creative week. In the spaces provided or in your journal, answer these questions as best as you can:

Which exercise did you enjoy most this week?

Why?

Was there any exercise this week that made you uncomfortable, and if so, which one?

Why do you think you felt this way?

Do you find that creativity and self-expression make you feel closer to God?

If so, how? If not, why not?

Is there any other form of creativity that you feel puts you in touch with God, and if so, what?

Were you inspired to try something new this week?

Are you continuing any exercises from the first two weeks?

Which ones?

What would you like to work on next week?

How do you feel about yourself right at this very moment?

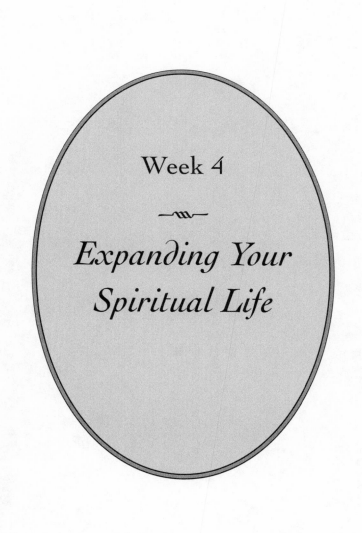

Week 4

Expanding Your
Spiritual Life

You're in the home stretch!

That's the good news.

The bad news is that, in some ways, this may be the most difficult week for you. Now that you've learned the fundamentals of being a spiritual person, you're going to put them into practice in a very concrete way. Call it a demonstration of faith, walking the walk, putting your money where your mouth is—just don't call it a day and end your journey here.

Though you're not going to be asked to do anything impossible or strenuous—we're not talking about climbing Mt. Everest here—you *will* be called upon to show your spiritual side in public through words and deeds. It may be a little weird at first. Family and friends will notice a change in you, if they haven't already, and you may have to explain your thirty-day quest.

But nobody ever said being spiritual is always easy—just more fulfilling. And what you do this week will have an effect on those around you. That's part of living a spiritual life too. We're all in this together.

Giving Yourself a Sabbath

"TGIF!" WE HOLLER as the shadows grow longer on Friday afternoon. We're free from job obligations, from alarm clocks and suits, take-out tuna sandwiches at the desk, traffic tie-ups on the freeway and delays on the train. We can take our minds and bodies away from the nine-to-five grind, go wherever, do whatever. Forty-eight hours of sheer bliss. Life is sweet.

So what do we do with that precious time? We do laundry, scrub the bathtub and mow the lawn. We circle the mall for a parking space and walk our feet off as we check out the sale at Old Navy (no, not the one on the west wing of the first floor, it's the one on the south wing of the second floor, but not the one next to the Starbucks, the one near the eyebrow-piercing place). We stand in line and pay outrageous fees for the latest action flick, only to miss half the dialogue because the guy behind us is shouting witticisms at the screen. Or we stay at home and zone out in front of the tube with the game or an old Michael J. Fox movie we've seen a few million times. Then, just when we've accomplished pretty much what we set out to do, it's nine-thirty on Sunday night, and our mind is already clicking back into Work Mode, wondering where those wonderful, perfect, blissful forty-eight hours went.

Fun? Sure. Hectic? Sometimes. Restful? No way.

We've been so conditioned to keep our minds and bodies always on the go that we don't stop even during the time we allot ourselves to take it easy. There's something that seems wrong about unwinding for its own sake. I'm as guilty as anyone. If Sunday night comes without my having seen a major exhibit at the Met, worked out at the gym for three hours or vacuumed every crumb from the rug, I wail, "I didn't get anything *done!*"

What I have to remind myself—and what we all should remember—is that rest for its own sake is not only a blessing but a necessity. Human beings may be able to function on a steady diet of stress and sensory stimulation, but we can't thrive on it for very long. Pretty soon, our bodies start to show the effects. We get sleepy. We become anxious and cranky. Our muscles clench into knots, our heart works harder, our stomach starts churning up acid. We cry, we snap, we fidget, we overeat, we pout. We sigh that life is passing us by. We berate ourselves for not doing enough. We look for new and better ways to keep ourselves active and entertained, even if they're not necessarily good for us.

What we don't do is give ourselves a real break, one that allows us to refresh our entire selves and come away renewed afterward. We don't give ourselves the opportunity to shut ourselves away from the working world and become reacquainted with ourselves and with God. But we can accomplish all that by returning to a very old, very beautiful tradition—the Sabbath.

The concept of designating one day in seven as a time of rest was considered so important that it was made one of the basic Ten Commandments in the Judeo-Christian theology for righteous living. Think about that for a minute. It's only logical that in any list of human laws, there would be clauses against murder, stealing, adultery and false witness against neighbors. Those are pretty big deals in anyone's book. Coveting other people's possessions—not a good thing, everyone should be happy with what they've got, and jealousy leads to hard feelings and fights—sure, that's a sin to avoid. Honoring your parents—maybe not as heinous as the others, but they're your parents, after all. And those first three, well, that's God explaining who the Higher Power is and how He wants to be treated. Never hurts to remind everyone that there's "something bigger than Phil," as Mel Brooks' Thousand-Year-Old Man used to say.

But not only are we commanded to "remember the Sabbath day," but we must also "keep it holy." It's not enough just to take a day off; we have to respect and hallow it by taking ourselves away from work—*all* work, even the tedious tasks we assign ourselves during our spare time.

So your next project is to take one day this week to give yourself a true Sabbath. Saturday or Sunday are ideal, of course, but if your schedule makes it easier for you to observe your rest on a weekday, go right ahead. The important thing is to give yourself the gift and stay as close as you can to the spirit of the commandment.

Start the day by spending a few minutes in prayer or meditation. If you ordinarily go to church or temple, do it. Those are terrific ways to separate yourself from the work week and feel calm from the inside out. But don't end your Sabbath there—keep the mood going. Do whatever makes you happiest and most relaxed. Read a book and don't stop until you finish the last page. Go for a long walk or a bike ride or a drive in the country. Try out a new recipe. Play the piano or paint or sing. Do the crossword puzzle. Do a little yoga. Feel like taking a delicious afternoon nap? Go for it! Want to shut the bedroom door and have a nooner? Nothing better!

Get the whole family involved. Read one of your favorite books aloud to the kids. Take out that Monopoly or Clue game you haven't touched in ages. Pick tomatoes together or have them help you plant marigolds. Spread a drop cloth over the dining room table or porch and create a huge collage with any odds and ends you have lying around. Introduce them to Bach or Ellington or the Righteous Brothers. Or just sit down and talk about anything at all.

Sure, there are some chores that are unavoidable. Kids have to be driven to soccer practice, the lunch dishes have to be washed, the kitchen floor has to be cleaned after the baby knocks a bowl of cereal on it. But try to keep those obligations to a minimum on your Sabbath. If you normally drop off your dry cleaning on Saturday morning, try doing it Friday instead. Think of chores as little thieves that steal away the time you've saved up for yourself. The more you can find ways to keep them from interfering with your day of rest, the happier you'll be at the end of the day. The dust will still be there on Monday morning. Trust me.

Now for the really killer part. Though the purpose of the Sabbath is to do what you enjoy most, there are a couple of fun activities I'm going to urge you to avoid. I'm not trying to be a wet blanket—there's a reason for this.

First, keep the TV off. No morning cartoons, no CNN headlines, no classic movies, no wrestling matches, not even wholesome family entertainment or religious sermons. The screen stays blank.

If that sounds like an awfully harsh rule for a day of rest, think about the part TV plays in your life. For many of us, relaxing at home usually means flopping on the sofa and switching on the tube. And if a few minutes turns into an hour or two, what of it? And what's wrong with channel-surfing an afternoon away, zoning out for a while just to escape from the cares of the week?

Zoning out is precisely the problem. TV rightly deserves its reputation as a mind-number. Entertaining images flicker in front of our eyes without our having to do anything, and it all goes by so fast that we have no chance to really process or contemplate it completely. It's a passive activity, so you can't control it or interact with it. You have no choice but to sit and take in whatever gets thrown at you. You can't be fully self-aware when your brain is being bombarded—and so, while you may think you're relaxing, you're not really renewing yourself from the inside out. If anything, turning on the TV means temporarily turning off a piece of your soul. No, no, of course I don't mean that the boob tube is the spawn of the underworld. But it's not spiritual, either.

Then there's the fact that watching television is an isolated—and isolating—activity. We pay so much attention to the screen that we block out everything else: sights, sounds, other people's needs, even our own needs. (If you doubt it, try calling a ten-year-old to dinner when he's engrossed in his favorite show.) Even when other people are in the room, we're not focusing on them. We're with them in body but certainly not in spirit. When was the last time you had a meaningful conversation with a family member while the TV was on? If someone starts talking during a favorite show, the usual response is: "You made me miss what Phoebe was saying!" As if an actor's videotaped punch line was more important than hearing what's on the mind of a friend or family member. The Sabbath should be the one day out of the week in which you're most in touch with yourself and your thoughts, and TV just doesn't allow that to happen.

And yeah, there's the whole issue of content. I'm not going to say that the sexual and violent images of many shows are solely responsible for the moral downfall of our country and the decay of our youth or that they should be banned altogether and replaced with continual reruns of *The Waltons*. There are some shows with risqué or violent content whose overall quality—the writing, acting or message—outweighs the objectionable portions. But I don't think they're altogether innocent, either. You can't be exposed to any idea or image for a long period of time and not be affected by it. In any event, an unvarying diet of anything is unhealthy, and that goes for TV, too.

There are no good excuses for not giving yourself a TV-free day. If there's something on during your Sabbath that you really want to watch, tape it for later or wait until the rerun. Go outside and shoot hoops or practice your curveball rather than holing up in the family room listening to the play-by-play. With the easy availability of video stores, there's virtually no such thing as a "can't-miss televised movie event" (viewers were popping *Titanic* tapes into their VCRs long before it was broadcast on cable).

Even if you're the only one in the family observing a personal Sabbath, try to get everyone else to cooperate on this point, too. Of course, the kids will protest. They'll get bored. They'll whine. They'll defy you and turn the TV on, anyway. But after a while, they'll adjust. They'll either find something else to occupy their time or else they'll learn that a little boredom won't kill them. They might even secretly find it a relief after a week packed with schoolwork and soccer games.

The same restriction applies to the computer. No Net-surfing or video games. I'm as guilty as anyone of losing myself in front of the monitor. But again, it's only slightly more interactive than watching TV. And when was the last time you got up from the keyboard or joystick saying, "Boy, do I feel refreshed now!"?

At least give it a try. You'll probably find that after a

while, you'll be enjoying your day off so much that you won't miss having the TV on.

The second thing I'd like you to avoid on your Sabbath is shopping. This one isn't a matter of isolationism or moral quandaries, and it has nothing to do with the act of spending. If you're out of milk, of course it's okay to run to the store for a half gallon—but if you want to keep to the letter of the rule, you might try to anticipate and take care of shortages like that before your day of rest begins.

What shopping does, whether you're just window-shopping at the mall or going on a genuine spree, is create a subtle sense of dissatisfaction. *What a great stereo system—I wish I could afford it. I could really use a long skirt in that color. I deserve a treat, don't I? Why can't I ever find anything I like?* We go in with a desire or a feeling of deprivation that we hope that stereo or skirt will ease. But as we all know, there is no one magical purchase that makes us feel so completely fulfilled that the desire for something new never comes back. There's always a better product waiting in the window.

There's nothing wrong with wanting things. Desire is a natural human emotion. But the Sabbath, of all times, should be a day for being aware of and grateful for what we already have—and who we already are. To realize: *I am not my possessions. What I have is not what I'm worth.*

So while you're giving yourself a break from mundane duties, give yourself a break from the constant pressure to buy stuff, too. (Think, too, about where a lot of that pressure is coming from—how many TV ads have you seen in your lifetime?) You might take an inventory of what you have now and realize how much you have already. Do you honestly have nothing to wear, or could you expand your wardrobe by finding new combinations of your existing shirts, pants and skirts, adding a sweater, tie or scarf? Is there anything in your house you've never used at all? Do you have any clothes, toys or appliances that might be put to better use in a school, library or shelter or given to a family who's recovering from a disaster or the aftermath of a war overseas?

Before you go to bed on your first Sabbath, make a mental list of all the things you have that you're thankful for. First, think of the items you've purchased in stores, then go over the ones that can't be bought at any price. That should give you an understanding of why your day of rest should include a break from shopping.

You may be saying to yourself right about now, "Who has time to spend a whole day relaxing? Other people may be able to afford that luxury, but not me." If that's your argument, then you might ask why you don't consider yourself important enough to treat yourself to that time off. If you can't be good to yourself on a regular basis, you can't truly be good to others, either. If nothing else, do it for your health. There are plenty of studies out there that confirm the medical benefits of de-stressing. It's good for your heart, your blood pressure, your immune system, your mind—and, yes, your soul, too.

It's a luxury you can't afford not to enjoy.

Being a Mitzvah Maker

A FEW YEARS AGO, someone came up with the slogan: "Practice random acts of kindness and senseless acts of beauty." It made a cute made-you-look bumper sticker, it sold a few T-shirts and, as is common in this hypercommunication age, the saying worked its way into standard usage.

But the best part about it all was that people actually started making it their business to practice those "random acts." A few even made it their primary mission. You'd hear their stories occasionally on the evening news or in upbeat newspaper columns. And admit it—you probably couldn't resist smiling when you heard about these unprompted good deeds, right? Maybe you were even tempted to hold a door for someone the next day, just to be nice.

Well, if you're looking to become a more spiritually oriented person, get ready to do more than just doorman duty. Because spirituality isn't just about your own relationship to God or your relationship to yourself, but about looking beyond yourself and serving others. To paraphrase Dickens's Marley, mankind is our business. We're not in this alone, and despite what governments and tabloids would have us believe, there is no one person who is more important than another. It's not enough just to coexist peacefully together as a planet; we have to help make life even a tiny bit easier for others on it.

This is nothing you don't already know, of course. All the major religious texts explain over and over again our obligation to love and help one another, and to give as good as we get. Jesus, Moses, Muhammad—they didn't gain such enormous followings by looking out for Number One. And would we have given Gandhi and Mother Teresa such an honored place in history if they hadn't devoted their lives to charity and service? Many wealthy persons may have received their fame through their money, but they have received honor and admiration for the way in which they use their millions to benefit others.

If, indeed, we are a reflection of God on earth, beings created to do His work, then good deeds are a large part of the equation. It doesn't matter how large or small they are; the fact that we consciously make the effort to help another person is an accomplishment in itself. (In Judaism, a good deed is called a *mitzvah*, which literally means "commandment." It's not just a nice gesture—it's a direct order from On High.)

You probably already do any number of nice little things throughout the average day: holding that door open, picking up some dropped item, giving directions to an out-of-towner, complimenting a colleague on her haircut. But these examples are the good-deed equivalent of no-brainers. Your coworker looks great, so you tell her so automatically. Someone drops a package behind you, it's almost a reflex reaction to turn around and retrieve it. And when a tourist asks the way to the art museum, what are you going to say—"Get out of my face"?

It takes more of an effort to decide to do something nice for someone or to go out of your way to do it. But those are the moments that make the headlines; that's what the bumper stickers are all about. And these are the deeds that make you feel best about yourself and more aware of your role as a spiritual person serving your fellow man. I've held my share of doors in my time, but that has never given me as much satisfaction as, say, the day I found the contents of a stolen wallet and mailed them back to their owner. Or sending a plant to my father-in-law for no other reason than he needed a pick-me-up. Or the coffee I bought for the elderly homeless man I used to pass on my way to work. He would always say, "Thank you so much," and the look in his eyes showed that he meant it.

So since this week is about reaching beyond yourself, then what better way to start than with this: At least three times in the next seven days, perform a deliberate random act of kindness—something that requires thought and effort on your part, an act that goes beyond an easy reaction to a situation. For instance, if you see someone fall down and hurt himself, it's nice to help him up. But to help him collect his things, get him something to drink, call an ambulance or a cab if necessary or get his phone number so you can call later to follow up—that's the kind of mitzvah I'm talking about.

To get you started, here are a few ideas:

· Take some of the extra tomatoes or zucchini from your garden and give it to a neighbor.
· Give money or a lunch to a homeless person, even if you suspect he or she is an alcoholic, drug abuser or phony.
· Let someone with a large cart of groceries go ahead of you or make up the difference if the person in front is short a few cents.
· Send a card for no particular reason.
· Offer to help cheer a crying child in a restaurant or on a bus, rather than glaring at the embarrassed parents.
· Donate old clothes, books or toys to charity, a hospital or a library.
· Send money to a disaster or war relief fund.
· Give your husband or wife a back rub without being asked.
· Watch a neighbor's house while they're away. Pick up their mail and newspapers; mow the lawn if the grass is getting too high.
· Slip a loving note into your child's notebook or lunch box.
· Give a candy bar to a coworker as an afternoon pick-me-up. Or bring in an extra cup of coffee for him or her when you arrive in the morning.

· Compliment a total stranger on his or her clothes, shoes, jewelry, hairstyle, smile.
· Next time you're on a plane or train and the person sitting next to you tries to engage you in conversation, don't pretend to be asleep or reading—join in. Sometimes people just need to be listened to.
· Take your dog out for an extra-long session of catch or give your cat a thorough brushing and back-scratching. Kindness to pets counts, too.
· Clip out interesting newspaper articles and send them to your parents.
· Call a friend you haven't seen in at least a year.
· Leave enough change at the newsstand to pay for the papers of the next three people behind you.
· Offer some good advice on an Internet message board.
· Be the one to initiate sex tonight.
· At the gym, let someone alternate sets with you on the weight machines, rather than making him or her wait while you do "just one more."
· If you receive outstanding service from anyone—say, a sales clerk, waiter, real estate agent, cabdriver or even the disembodied voice of a customer-service representative—find out who his or her supervisor is and write a complimentary letter, explaining specifically how this person helped you. This could mean a lot when yearly review time rolls around. And in the case of a waiter or server, leaving a generous tip would also be appreciated.
· The same goes for professionals. Doctors, nurses and

dentists like to hear they're doing a good job, too. Write a thank-you letter.

I'M SURE you can come up with some creative ideas of your own. The nice thing about doing good deeds is that the more you do, the better you feel afterward—and the more you want to do them.

And sometimes you don't know what kind of effect an act of kindness has on someone else. One compliment can make a person's day, and that cheer may be passed on to others. That word of encouragement in your child's lunch box could sustain him or her through a tough chemistry test. The woman who gets that free newspaper might turn around and pay for another stranger's *USA Today*. Soothing that crying child might keep a parent at the end of his rope from hitting the toddler.

No matter what you decide to do or who you decide will be the recipient of your kind deed, the messages you send are the same: *I acknowledge you. In this moment, you are important to me, and you are always an important person in this world. There should be good in your life. You deserve to have something nice happen to you.*

Those are messages we can't hear often enough. And if we expect to hear them from God, we'd better start giving as good as we get.

Thou Shalt Not Gossip

SO FAR, most of these spiritual exercises have been pretty positive ones: projects to enhance your awareness, open your soul, bring you closer to your family and community. I haven't been giving you any "thou shalt nots." You knew it was too good to last. I'm about to give you one now.

There's something about us humans that seems to revel in a sense of superiority over others. Maybe it's because there are so many of us that we're afraid we'll get lost in anonymity if we don't establish ourselves as being better than everyone else in some way. Maybe we're concerned with taking the peremptory strike before someone discovers our own flaws. Or maybe there's just a gene for cruelty woven in the strands of our DNA, never to be bred out. If there is, it must be a uniquely human gene—you never see a dog laughing at another dog because he happens to be a Chihuahua rather than a Rottweiler. Or a blue jay smirking at an eagle for having such drab feathers.

Whatever the reason, we have an unfortunate tendency to speak ill of others at every given opportunity. At work, we gripe about our colleagues or the boss: "He's so clueless!" "She doesn't pull her weight around here." "I hate his attitude." With friends, we share gossip about people we know: "What does she see in him, anyway?" "I can't believe how insensitive he was." With family, we carp and criticize: "Can't you keep your room neat?" "You never listen to me." "You're spending too much."

It's become so much of a habit that we can't help making negative snap judgments even about the strangers we pass on the street. Admit it—you've sneered at someone wearing a mismatched or too-tight outfit. Or pitied someone whose teeth or hair or nose didn't look like a supermodel's. Or seen an overweight person licking an ice cream cone and automatically thought: *That's the* last *thing that pig should be eating.*

Gossip and slander make up a large part of what we consider entertainment. The weekly tabloids and entertainment magazines turn a profit out of our curiosity over the careers, love lives, divorces, money problems and quarrels among celebrities we don't know personally. On the "confrontational" talk shows, guests scream insults at each other as audience members rush to stick in their opinions: "Kick that guy to the curb!" "Start treating your mother with some respect!" "Your baby deserves a loving father!"

During prime time, even the shows noted for the quality of their writing and acting feature kids who mouth off at their parents, couples tossing sarcastic digs at each other while they fix dinner, colleagues trading witty insults about their appearance and innuendos about their sex lives. We're invited to share a laugh of ridicule at home videos of everyday people falling off ladders, horses and skis or losing their pants at inopportune moments.

The trouble with this daily onslaught of jabs and zingers is that it makes us numb to the verbal pain we inflict on others. Contrary to the familiar taunt, words *can* hurt us. We feel more vulnerable, our frailties exposed. We become inferior in someone else's eyes. A steady diet of insults, criticism and gossip slowly erodes our confidence and self-esteem like the ocean creating sand out of what once were huge boulders.

The Talmud teaches that idle gossip isn't just cruel—it's actually sinful. Doing wrong to your fellow man in any way, even merely through words, is an injustice that cannot be tolerated. Not to mention the fact that it goes against every rule of spiritual living. You can't be at peace with yourself or with God if you're attacking someone else. You can't ask blessings for yourself in one breath and curse someone else the next.

So that brings us to the next assignment. For two days a week, resolve not to say or listen to anything negative about anyone. And that means everyone—your family, your friends, your boss, people you really hate, the President, Julia Roberts.

No, it won't be easy. You'll find yourself stopping in midsentence a lot ("Did you hear what he . . . ?"). You'll have to find an excuse to walk away when the conversation turns catty. You'll need to put aside some of your favorite magazines for another day. You'll have to force yourself to look at that obese man with the ice cream cone and think: *Ooh, that looks good. I could go for some Cherry Garcia myself.* And when you find yourself getting mad at the husband who forgets to take out the trash or the child who brings home a bad report card, you'll have to find other ways of expressing yourself other than: "You can't even do the simplest things around the house!" or "I'm sick of you slacking off!"

Once you've gotten into the habit of thinking before you speak, then it's time to go a step further. It's not just enough to curb your own hurtful tongue—try keeping other people from doing it, too. So when your best friend from work starts trashing your cubicle mate, come back with something positive: "She really helped me out when I was backed up with projects." Or say flat-out, "I don't feel comfortable talking about anyone behind his back, if you don't mind." Or simply find a new topic of conversation. If your child complains about a classmate, you could say: "I know he hurt your feelings, but we don't call anyone a 'jerk' in this house."

I know this may seem like a Pollyannaish kind of assignment. You might worry or feel embarrassed that other people might find out about your attempts to curb slander and gossip. *They're going to think I'm some kind of goody-goody!* And that's rather sad when you think about it. We've become so used to trash talk and rumor-spread-ing that it seems abnormal not to join in. You're considered weird if you don't rush to blacken someone's reputation or share a juicy story that may or may not be true.

There's a classic fairy tale about two sisters, a kind one and a cruel one, who each meet an old beggar woman. True to form, the kind one takes the woman in for the night, feeds her and gives her what little she has, while the cruel one spits at the beggar and passes her by. Naturally, the crone turns out to be a witch in disguise (there must be some kind of contractual obligation in these stories about sorceresses going incognito), and she casts a spell on the two sisters. The good sister is blessed: Whenever she speaks, precious gems fall from her lips. The bad one is cursed, forever doomed to spew spiders and snakes every time she opens her mouth. From that day on, the evil sibling is hated and feared, while the kindhearted one has nothing but friends, a comfortable lifestyle and, of course, the standard-issue handsome prince.

I don't know about you, but given the choice, I'd rather speak in rubies and emeralds. They're a lot more pleasant to look at, and they tend to get you much farther in life.

Allowing Yourself to Forgive

SOMETIMES IT'S HARDER to tell someone, "I forgive you," than it is to say, "I'm sorry." An apology, after all, is a submissive act. You're the one who's asking for absolution, the one who can't rest until your guilt and remorse are removed. You're at the mercy of somebody else, your heart on the line, waiting to be restored to glory in that person's eyes.

On the other hand, there's something so wonderfully powerful about refusing to accept another person's atonement. You can keep your anger in full flaming passion, which can sustain you long after you've forgotten exactly why you're so mad in the first place. You can milk every last drop of public sympathy in your role as the proud, righteous Wounded Victim. You can even have the satisfaction of knowing that as long as you stand your ground, the person who did you wrong is a lesser human being. He's a soul smudged by that one sin that has yet to be washed away on earth—and you're the one with the scrub brush.

But the trouble with grudges is that they can severely sap you of your inner peace, and they go against every spiritual ideal. We say that we "carry" a grudge, and with good reason. It's a huge burden on your soul as well as your mind. When you have to lug your grudge around for days or weeks or years or decades on end, it tends to get heavier rather than lighter, and the forgiving harder and harder to do, until the relationship is flooded with so much hurt and resentment that there's no going back. It's difficult to move forward as an individual when you've got that kind of anchor keeping you weighted to the past. So in a sense, it's as if that person is causing more damage than he actually did.

It's not easy by any means, but people can forgive each other for enormous wrongs. Wives and husbands forgive affairs. Parents forgive children who say hurtful things. Friends accept apologies for borrowed items that have been lost. Divorced people find it in their hearts to forgive whatever their ex did to end the marriage.

A couple of years ago, I interviewed someone who exemplifies both courage and forgiveness. Shortly before she was scheduled to compete in the 1994 Winter Olympics, American ice dancing champion Elizabeth Punsalan learned that her brother, who had battled schizophrenia for years, had killed their father after being released from a psychiatric hospital. She could have chosen to bury herself in rage and sorrow and refuse to speak to her brother ever again. But she didn't. Instead, bolstered by the support of her family and by Jerod Swallow, her husband and skating partner, she found it within herself to make her peace with her brother. It was the only way, she told me, that she could go on with her life. And so she did, going on to win more medals and a top-ten final placement at the 1998 Olympics.

Is there someone in your life you're furious at right now? Someone you're not speaking to? Someone you've vowed never to forgive? This exercise is for you. Hard as it may be, you're going to have to at least start planting the seeds of forgiveness. Even if you were absolutely, without-a-doubt right and he was totally, undeniably wrong, you're not going to be a happier person for holding that against him.

First, close your eyes and imagine that person sitting in front of you. Imagine him or her saying, "I'm so sorry. Can you ever forgive me?" (Never mind if the person would never say that in real life; this is a visualization and you can do whatever you like within it.) Now picture yourself saying, "I forgive you"—and meaning it. Say it again. Say it as many times as it takes until you can honestly believe it. Now picture your anger at that person as a huge boulder over your heart. Feel its weight. Then make that boulder gradually dissolve until all that's left is dust. Make that dust trickle through your body from your head down to your feet and out through your toes. Breathe deeply a few times and feel how light your heart is now.

The next step, if you have the courage to take it, is to

find closure in person. If the person who wronged you has already apologized, call or write him and say, "I forgive you." If he hasn't, consider making the first move. Use that call or letter to say, "I don't want this to come between us. Can't we find a way to get past this hurt?" But if you just can't deal with an actual confrontation, then focus on living without the grudge. You've forgiven that person in your heart; now it's time to move on.

Let me clarify something, though: Forgiving someone doesn't mean forgetting the deed. We have to remember the things that pass between us and others, even the painful ones, in order to avoid repeating the same mistakes. And I'm not asking you to welcome back with open arms the one who wronged you. There are some people whom you must keep out of your life—abusers, molesters, addicts who hurt others with their addictions, people who drain your energy and money.

What forgiveness does mean, however, is that you're allowing yourself to move beyond that strength-sapping hatred and hurt feelings, to free yourself from the time-consuming task of nursing the resentment. Then you can spend that time in more productive, life-affirming ways.

Grudges don't bring out the best in us. Forgiveness does.

Rites of Passage

I'LL NEVER FORGET the evening when the rabbi handed me the velvet-covered Torah scrolls and led me down the aisles of the temple. I was aware of my friends and family as they touched the scroll cover with their prayerbooks, but their faces melded together into one big smile of pride. Then before I knew it, I was back on the bimah (altar), the scrolls were open, and I started to chant the Hebrew words written thousands of years ago, using the silver pointer my husband had given me as a gift to commemorate the happy occasion.

As I said before, I didn't suddenly transform into a different person or even a more religious one. But something happened up there that's hard to describe. There was excitement, yes. And pride at being able to accomplish such a major feat. And, yeah, a little relief when I got through my Torah and Haftarah portions with no noticeable problems. Yet it was more than that. In those few minutes, I had made a commitment to my faith and my people. I had publicly chosen to be a full-fledged part of a tradition that dated back farther than I could even imagine. Still more than that, I had finally graduated from the stubborn child who rejected her family's values and stepped into a womanhood of learning, responsibility and searching for truth.

Rites of passage are so much a part of our lives that we sometimes forget to acknowledge how vital they are. We blow out candles on birthday cakes, put on caps and gowns, slip rings on fingers, throw dirt on coffins, but we don't always stop to reflect what the rites mean to us, where we've come from or where we're going to next.

THESE CEREMONIES hallow the particular moment in time, but they also hallow who we are as people. We're not the same once we turn sixteen or forty or seventy. We leave a part of us behind when we finish school or commit our lives to another person, and we look ahead to a future that will be affected by the changes we have just made. We honor our uniqueness and our place in a world we often don't understand, and we ask witnesses to join us so that our passage will be remembered and spoken of for generations to come.

Today, start thinking of a rite of passage ceremony you could perform for yourself. The commemoration might be something obvious or traditional: turning thirty; going through a confirmation or bat mitzvah again; leaving or starting a job; having a child or grandchild.

Or come up with a passage that's unusual and

uniquely you: Coloring your first gray hair—or deciding to go gray with style. Your first new (nonused) car. Paying off the mortgage. Starting to learn a new skill (never again will you not know how to swim/make the perfect crepe/speak conversational Italian/create a Web page). Finishing the complete works of Dostoevsky or Jane Austen. Writing the first page of your first book. Maybe you'd like to observe the Jewish tradition of honoring the new moon, recognizing the mystical bond your own body has with the waxing and waning of this celestial one.

Don't forget the rest of your family, either. Maybe your husband, wife or partner lost enough weight to need a new wardrobe. Your child just got the training wheels off his bike, lost his last baby tooth, became the "big brother" or gave up—all by himself—the blanket he carried around until it threatened to become nothing but filthy blanket molecules. Your daughter got her period. Your mother went on her first date since the divorce.

You might even want to find a group of friends who are all going through a similar commencement, such as menopause, first babies or children all going to college for the first time. Some women choose to have a "croning" ceremony to honor the wisdom that comes only with age. If you're a little younger than standard crone age, then get your old friends together and celebrate your tenth or twentieth year away from high school or college—do something special to honor the friendship between you rather than peering at nametags of classmates you barely knew.

Once you've decided what to do, there are as many

ways to celebrate as there are reasons to do it. It could be as simple as lighting a candle one night or as elaborate as a party for all your family and friends. Use your imagination. Find a hill to climb and watch the sun rise. Announce it in a chat room. Write a letter to yourself or to all your loved ones, thanking them for helping you reach this important moment in your life. Write a poem or a speech for the honoree or, better yet, have her create the poem herself and read it to the family.

Say a prayer in your church, temple or mosque. Make a contribution to an appropriate charity. Start a scrapbook, guestbook or journal. Make the loved one's favorite meal or take him for a "just-us-two" night with dinner or a movie. You could create an altar of images representing the passage—pictures, certificates, report cards, photos clipped from magazines.

Have everyone make up lyrics to a popular tune and sing it to the guest of honor. Create a list of top ten reasons this passage is so important. Think of something you're leaving behind in this process and give it a formal backyard burial, complete with eulogy and *Taps*. (For a child entering high school, perhaps you could lay a toy to rest; for a change of career, your old business cards; for menopause, a pack of birth control pills.) Or simply lavish the honoree with plenty of hugs, kisses and shouts of "I'm so proud of you!"

Be sure, though, to find a way to acknowledge who you were before now and what you'll be afterward. You might write in your spirituality journal: "I now say goodbye to the self who believed she would never find her dream job. I love the person she was, but I also honor the courage and determination within myself that allowed me to reach past my fears and achieve this goal. Now I look ahead to a joyous time as I pursue the career I always wanted. May I continue to grow in knowledge, strength and wisdom."

When we stop to remember these special times, we also become aware once again of our place within the universe. We have only a finite time on this earth, and in this brief period, we continue to change, to grow and to become better people in ways large and small. Sometimes it takes a moment of reflection to allow us to realize how far we've come and how far we have yet to go.

Reclaiming Rituals

A POP QUIZ: What do these activities have in common?

Brushing your teeth before bed
Having a pick-me-up candy bar at four o'clock every day
Going out with your best friends one night a month
Trimming the Christmas tree

THESE ARE ALL common examples of rituals—the little acts we perform daily, weekly, yearly and at other times to give us comfort and security.

Our need for ritual begins virtually from the moment we exit the womb. As babies, we come to know that we can expect to be fed at certain hours of the day. The feeling of physical satisfaction leads us to recognize our personal needs and understand that someone will meet them, and every time our hunger is sated makes us a little more confident in the predictability of life.

Then we become toddlers, learning that there's a huge world that extends far beyond our crib. We run, we explore, we demand, we discover. Yet, precisely because the world is such an enormous place, we need certain constants in our lives to reassure us that there's an order and a safety there, too, and people we can rely on. That's why young children refuse to eat anything but mashed potatoes and jelly, why they wake you up at 6 A.M. even on weekends, and why they have to hear *Goodnight Moon* three times and "Night-night, sweetie" twice and have their ratty old teddy bear exactly on the left side of the bed before they can even think about falling asleep.

We may outgrow the teddy bear and the picture books, but our need for ritual stays constant even as adults. Why else do we designate Thursday nights as "Must-See TV"? Why do we get upset if something happens to disrupt our morning routine? And why do couples argue over where to spend Thanksgiving, whether to make chestnut or sausage stuffing and how much cinnamon to put in the pumpkin pie?

Rituals keep our lives in balance. And when the rites are put into a spiritual context, they can help make us more aware of our relationship to God. Think of all the little routines that go on in just one hour at a house of worship—most of them activities that we don't ordinarily do anywhere else. We endow the motions with meaning and, once again, sanctify a moment in time.

So AS YOU might have guessed, one of your assignments for this week is to perform a spiritual ritual at least once.

(You'll probably find yourself trying a couple more than that.) It can be something unique to your religious faith. It could be something taken from a different religion. Or it could be something you make up yourself—as long as it's done in an appropriately worshipful manner. Here are some ideas to get you started:

· Light a candle as you say a prayer of your choice. Notice how it immediately creates a hushed and awe-filled atmosphere in the room. Reflect on it for at least ten minutes before blowing it out. Or buy a yahrzeit (twenty-four-hour memorial) candle and keep it lit the entire day in honor of a loved one who has passed on. Or light a candle in church.
· Say a blessing before dinner—either a familiar one or one you create yourself. Then be mindful of the goodness of the food as you eat.
· Say a rosary at home.
· Kneel toward Mecca.
· Light incense.
· Burn a smudge stick (available at herb stores and spiritual shops). Native Americans traditionally burn dried sage and wave it around the corners of a room to cleanse it and drive out evil spirits.
· Tape a copy of the Lord's Prayer or the Twenty-third Psalm to your dashboard and read it before you start the car.
· Hang a mezuzah on the doorpost of your house. Touch it and kiss your fingers when you enter or leave.
· Give up something you like for Lent.

· Give up food and water (if your health permits) for Yom Kippur.
· Don't eat until sundown during Ramadan.
· Designate one dinner a week as "Spiritual Night" and talk about biblical stories, miracles, moral issues and other related topics around the table.
· Make the sign of the cross as you pass a church or cemetery.
· Say, "Thank You, God," the moment you wake up.
· Make a charity jar and drop your loose change into it when you come home from work.
· Think of someone who is ill, hurt or in mental pain and spend a few minutes sending thoughts of healing her way.
· Bless your children before they go to school, before bedtime or when they have something important coming up, like a big test, a game or a school dance.
· Buy and use a miniature Zen garden. (It consists of a board filled with sand, several stones and a rake. Arrange the stones and sand to your satisfaction as you meditate.)
· Hang a dream catcher from your window and notice whether you sleep better at night.
· Read a Bible story out loud with your family.
· Say a small prayer of protection before going on vacation or business trips. Bless bread and wine before your Sabbath dinner.
· Find a church close to your workplace and sit in the pew for a few minutes during lunch hour.
· Buy a new book on spirituality once a month.

- Research a holiday from your particular faith that you don't ordinarily celebrate—be it Maundy Thursday, Simchat Torah or Diwali—and observe it this year.
- Find a meditation maze and walk through it, concentrating on the journey rather than the end.

I have a mezuzah on my front door. It's often described as a "Jewish amulet." Inside, it contains a portion of Deuteronomy, which says, "Thou shalt love the Lord thy God with all thy heart, with all thy soul and with all thy might. And these words which I command you this day you shall teach to your children. You shall speak of them when you lie down and when you rise up, when you go out and when you go in . . ." I make it a point to touch the mezuzah when I leave the house, and it reminds me to be thankful for the day ahead, and to be careful as I travel to keep myself and others safe.

I also have one on my bedroom door (they're for all the doorposts in your house, except the bathroom), and I touch it before I go to bed, bringing my fingers to my lips. It reminds me to be grateful for all the gifts of the day, to be thankful for my friends and family and for the gifts of my life.

*—*KATHERINE WERTHEIM

Do It in Groups

THE TRADITION of gathering two or more people together to discuss important topics is as old as mankind itself. Back when there were no newspapers, self-help books or therapists, all our ancestors had was each other to relay recent events, bring problems to the fore and express opinions.

Over the years, we've modified the tradition in any number of ways to suit our purposes—town meetings, press conferences, couples' therapy, support groups, fan clubs—but the basic idea is still the same. Part of being fully human is expressing our ideas and feelings and arranging an organized forum allows us all to have our say in an orderly and civilized fashion. Where spirituality is concerned, practicing privately without sharing our ideas is certainly an option. But many people feel the need to go farther than that—they don't want to make the journey alone.

The concept of spirituality groups isn't new, either. In addition to formal worship services, there are church and temple sisterhoods, Bible study meetings, campus religious organizations, socials for singles and married couples, tent revivals and so on. And if you already belong to a group you're comfortable with, you may not need this next exercise. But if you don't, I strongly urge you to try it: creating your own spirituality circle.

Forming a group can help you grow in your faith and beliefs while at the same time helping others grow in theirs. In a safe and welcoming environment, you can talk, laugh, read, sing, celebrate, mourn, contemplate and support—and come away a little wiser, a little more enlightened, perhaps a little more open-minded and ideally more sure of your spiritual self.

Start by asking a few trusted friends to join you one afternoon or evening a month. You might ask each one to bring another friend who they think would benefit from participating. Depending on what you want to get out of your group, you might choose men or women who share your particular beliefs, or perhaps select friends from a variety of religious backgrounds and degrees of faith. Try for a mix of ages and ethnicities, if you can—this will make your discussions that much more layered and interesting.

Make your first meeting low-key. Have it at your home to start (others in the group can host the meetings later on), and keep it to a couple of hours, starting with one topic of discussion (or a reading from a holy book) and letting it go on from there.

Sally Craig and Robin Deen Carnes, the authors of *Sacred Circles: A Guide to Creating Your Own Women's*

Spirituality Group, recommend starting every meeting by setting the proper mood. Dim or turn off the lamps and light candles instead. Use incense, aromatic oils or smudge sticks to make the atmosphere even more calming and pleasant. Open the session with a prayer—either a standard favorite or one created by you or another group member. Or start with a minute or two of silence so that you can drink in one another's presence and feel a sense of community.

The host for each session should set the tone for the evening and act as a moderator for discussions. Through trial and error, you'll discover what works for you. You may want to go around the room and have everyone talk in turn to ensure that no one feels left out, or else you might try the Native American tradition of the "talking stick." The stick (or any other significant item you can find) is passed around the circle, and whoever holds it may speak whatever is on his or her mind as the rest of the crowd listens quietly without interrupting. When the speaker finishes, the stick is passed to anyone else who wishes to have a say.

Above all, your group should be a haven where everyone feels free to express themselves without feeling constrained or condemned. So while lively debate and discussion is encouraged, criticism, insults and judgmental remarks are not. You'll probably learn some very personal things about the members of the group as you get to know one another, too. But whatever is said within the circle should stay there, otherwise you risk losing the vital atmosphere of trust.

Once you have your group together, what should you talk about? You're limited only by your imagination.

Because this is a spiritually based group, you'll probably want to do some analyses of the Bible, Torah or other holy or spiritual books. But that's just for starters.

You could also:

· discuss topics such as spirituality in nature, faith in everyday life, marriage, children, sex, love, parents . . . or the exercises in this book
· write prayers
· compose songs
· draw pictures
· remember loved ones
· create your own altars
· celebrate Rosh Chodesh, the new moon
· celebrate the changing of the seasons
· honor a member going through an important life change
· choose animal totems for yourselves that represent the qualities you would most like to embody
· create a ritual dinner

EXPERIMENT. Have fun. Learn. Whatever feels right to the members of your circle will help guide you as the months go on.

You might be pleasantly surprised by the things you learn from people you thought you knew pretty well. They may come to view you in a new light, too. And with any luck, you'll come away from each meeting either learning something different about yourself or calmer and more certain of your personal link to God.

Your Spiritual Workplace

THIS CHAPTER probably looks out of place to you. After all, unless you're a member of the clergy or one of the cast of *Touched by an Angel*, you probably don't think of the workplace as being a place to find anything even remotely resembling a Higher Power. It's a place for long hours that usually cut into whatever time you'd rather spend doing things you enjoy more. It's often fatiguing and stressful. You perform mundane, repetitive or high-pressure tasks. You try to impress your supervisors and simultaneously get along with a crew of people you might not necessarily choose as friends. And the weekends and holidays almost inevitably come as a welcome relief.

But spirituality, as you know by now, isn't restricted to weekend hours. God doesn't take a coffee break and leave you to your own devices during those eight or twelve hours you spend at the office or store, restaurant or hospital. And you can't stop living by spiritual principles just because you happen to be on the job—quite the contrary. Since so many of us define ourselves at least in part by our careers, it's all the more important to incorporate our belief systems into that portion of our lives.

So starting today, you're going to start looking at your workplace as a holy place.

We'll start with the easy part: setting the atmosphere. True, an office or workstation isn't a cathedral, so there's only so much you can do to establish it as a place where you can allow a Higher Spirit to enter. Fortunately, though, you don't have to do very much at all. Start by setting up a small workspace altar for yourself. Depending on your company's policies, you may not be allowed to display overly religious items like crosses or statues, but apart from that, use your imagination.

Take a couple of framed pictures, either of your family or of a scene that you find especially relaxing or inspiring, and arrange them facing you. If your employer permits it, you could put a significant object on top of your computer monitor, such as a beautiful stone, a shell or a small stuffed toy. Buy a miniature meditation garden and arrange the stones and sand in a way that makes you feel peaceful. In my office (where, fortunately, tasteful creativity is not discouraged), I've set aside space on my bulletin board for items like photos, postcards of famous paintings and a few key chains shaped like famous board games (to remind myself that nine-to-six life has to be fun sometimes). Or you could just bring in a potted plant as a reminder that beauty, growth and creation are always around us.

If you don't have the luxury of a desk, use your locker or bulletin board. If you have no designated workspace at all, try putting something in your pocket—say, a copy of the Twenty-third Psalm, your child's drawing, a bright autumn leaf or a piece of soft velvet you can touch. The point is to have a place you can turn to for just a few moments every day at work to counteract the tension or keep it from escalating.

Look at your object or altar—or touch it, if you like—and reflect for a minute or two about what it means to you. Then close your eyes and take a few deep breaths, making sure to let your stomach expand as you inhale and contract as you exhale. Roll your neck slowly in a circle to the right, then to your left. Check your shoulders for tension. (I know that mine tend to hunch up around my ears.) Then you can open your eyes and go on your way.

Another obvious way to bring spirituality to the job is to pray. Most employers don't permit loud or intrusive displays of religious expression that might make coworkers uncomfortable, but few would object to your closing your eyes for a few moments before starting work and asking God for an enjoyable and productive day. (You could do this on the commute to work, too.) If I have to make a difficult phone call—say, rejecting a writer's article—I often find myself thinking: *God, help me to say the right thing.* It makes me feel less alone when I pick up the receiver.

In the interest of keeping employees happy and motivated, some businesses even permit workers to hold on-site Bible or religious study sessions during lunchtime. If yours isn't one of them (you might try broaching the subject with your boss or human resources department), you could always find a like-minded coworker and set a monthly lunch date to get together and talk about faith issues.

There's also the issue of keeping to your personal convictions when it comes to being on the job during a time you believe you shouldn't be working. Naturally, there are times when it may be simply unavoidable, and some employers are less flexible than others. But when it comes to, say, the urge to go into the office just to "get a few things done" on the day you would normally observe your Sabbath, you might want to think about your priorities. Will the work be any better for having been done a day earlier, or would it be better for you to take the downtime with God and renew yourself before plunging back into the workday grind?

Some years ago, I used to report to the office on mornings when Rosh Hashanah and Yom Kippur, the Jewish High Holy Days, fell on weekdays. I thought I was being a devoted employee and that missing one or two days of work for religious reasons might be looked at as either overly pious or self-indulgent. But even as I tried to concentrate on my work, there was a part of me that wished I were in a temple singing and reflecting on the past year. Even though I didn't consider myself the least bit observant, my soul was still being called to put this holy time of year above my job and salary. Now I attend services on both days regardless of when they fall. After all, the great Dodgers pitcher Sandy Koufax refused to play in the

World Series on Yom Kippur. I doubt I'll ever do anything nearly as crucial in my workplace as going for the pennant.

But all these are relatively minor issues. Being spiritual at work has more to do with the way you present yourself and the way you act toward others. If you think about it, most of us have two separate personalities: our work persona and the nonwork one. There are certain basic differences, of course. On the job, we wear a certain style of clothing. We report to one or more people or supervise an assistant or staff or both. We keep to certain workplace rules of decorum.

But above and beyond that, our "work selves" sometimes behave in ways contrary to our better judgment— ways we might not tolerate in ourselves outside of the job. We might habitually show up late, leave early or sneak extra time into the lunch hour or coffee break. We might take home small office supplies because "no one will miss them," copy personal documents on company equipment or abuse the office e-mail by using it to forward the latest scary Net rumor.

Sometimes we behave unspiritually when we don't treat the people at work with respect. We become argumentative, condescending, impatient. We criticize a colleague's performance without finding out the source of the problem or working out ways to make things better. We spread office gossip without finding out the truth first or considering the possible hurt it might do to everyone involved. We forget that our supervisors are only human, our assistants aren't servants, our customers, clients and patients honestly do need our help and the people on the bottom rung of the company are the ones who could be on their way up in a few years—while we're on our way down.

We also do a disservice to ourselves, spiritually speaking, when we don't try to put our best effort into our work every day—and when we don't try to establish ourselves in a career in which we feel we can make a difference. Some of us are guilty of being driven to succeed to the exclusion of family, friends and other important priorities; some of us find fault with everything about our job, when the true fault lies with our own attitude.

Does any of this sound familiar? Does your work persona seem at odds with the person you are after five o'clock? Then try this "as if" exercise. Actors do this all the time to help them get inside their characters without feeling false or constrained; since you're trying to change your role at work, it can work here, too.

When you go to work tomorrow, ask yourself periodically throughout the day: *What would a spiritual person do now? Am I acting as if I were living by God-centered principles?* Clearly, someone trying to draw closer to his or her Higher Power would resist the temptation to sneak home that extra box of ballpoint pens. You can also remind yourself to behave in a more spiritually oriented way just before meetings, phone calls, reviews and conferences.

Some Christians use a similar strategy to handle problems and ethical dilemmas, asking themselves, *What would Jesus do?* and then going by the choice they believe Jesus himself would make in that situation. What I'm suggesting here is slightly different, however. There's a Jewish aphorism: When our lives are called into account, God will not ask us, "Why weren't you as great as Moses?" Rather, He will ask, "Why weren't you as great as *you*?" We all have the ability to live up to our highest individual ideals, and yet we don't always aim that high.

So as you go about your day, do frequent self-checks. Are you working up to your capacity? Are you taking care of priority projects rather than pushing them to the side for "later"? Would you be proud to tell your Higher Power about the work you did and the way in which you handled it?

Think, too, of the people you come into contact with every day. Nobody's asking you to be friends with everyone in the workplace. You don't even have to like them. But like it or not, they're with you forty hours a week, and they deserve the best from you, too. That means showing respect at all times, asking rather than demanding, staying calm in the face of rudeness or criticism (apart from quietly correcting mistakes for the sake of justice) and fighting the urge to complain or gossip about any coworkers behind their backs.

If you work in a field in which you give service to others, remember that service is a very spiritual concept and that every client or customer deserves equal consideration. It's the old Golden Rule in effect: If you want to be treated well, you have to treat others well first. Would you want to be known as the cold and impassive doctor, the surly waiter, the bored salesperson, the sleazy Realtor?

It may help to remember that regardless of how your

background and experience differs from that of your coworkers', you all have much in common. You all get up far too early, probably on too little sleep. You all face nightmarish traffic and cramped trains. Your boss gets headaches, runs in her hose and gets her feet wet in the rain just as much as you do. And everyone in your place of business feels like singing for joy when Friday afternoon rolls around.

Sometimes it takes personal crises to see how human and vulnerable even a coworker can be. I've seen people I've worked with cope with divorce, hurry home to care for a sick child, worry over an unemployed spouse, miss work to bury a parent. Some have become seriously ill themselves or even died. When home life intrudes into work life, it puts things into perspective and makes us realize that some things are more important than closing a deal, making a sale, breaking a record or (yes) publishing a book.

At least once this week, go through your day at work looking at your colleagues as you imagine a Spirit would. Try hard to see them not as tyrants, slackers or even friends, but as individual souls struggling to find their way in the world and handling their own problems as best they can. If your supervisor snaps at you, don't seethe at him—it's possible that someone might have snapped at him an hour ago. The woman who always drops by your cubicle to complain about something might be desperate for someone to listen. And the colleague who seems inattentive during your meeting might be feeling the effects of an anxious night taking the family dog to the animal hospital.

Knowing that, it should be easier to deal with them fairly and kindly, just as a Higher Spirit would. Again, it's not necessary to become the best friend of everyone at work, but it's important not to behave as if they were your worst enemies, either. Your own attitude has a lot to do with the way others react to you—it's easier to get on the case of an employee who appears surly or uninterested than it is to shout at one who's pleasant and at least trying to understand where you're coming from.

Does that mean you have to be a saint or a doormat? Absolutely not. There are times when you have to stand up for yourself at work. But again, in keeping with your spiritual nature, you can make your point without making anyone else's life difficult.

For example, when a coworker gives you grief over an incident, you can employ the techniques marriage therapists recommend for warring couples. Acknowledge the other person's feelings ("I know this upset you"), reiterate the problem ("You're upset because I didn't complete the report yesterday") and explain what you'll do to solve the problem and prevent it from happening in the future ("I'll finish the report by noon today, and I'll rearrange my duties to allow me to have the reports in by the fifteenth of each month").

Finally, spirituality at work means acknowledging the contributions you do and taking pride in them. In every line of work, every job is significant in some way, and they all come together to make the workplace run. A hospital needs its orderlies as much as its surgeons. Corporations rely on their mailroom staffs to get important documents into the right hands promptly.

Whenever I hit a rough spot at work, I think about everything I've done for the magazine in my thirteen-plus-year career. I've edited hundreds of stories, polished tens of thousands of sentences. I've written a couple of dozen articles that readers never would have seen otherwise. I've helped women get their stories told, which in turn have been seen by millions of people. And though I may not know it, the articles I've edited and written may have given thousands of readers the information they needed to improve their lives, marriages and health. Maybe I gave someone a much-deserved laugh after a rough day. Maybe a story I edited on relationships helped someone patch up her marriage. Maybe a human-interest story I wrote inspired a reader to volunteer her time or money or take steps to help someone else or to follow a dream.

Think of all the things you've accomplished in the course of your career. Chances are you've touched a lot of lives, too. You've made them just a little easier, a little happier, a little wiser. Now imagine how many lives have been touched by the people you've dealt with, and you'll see how much of a ripple effect even the smallest gesture can have.

You—and the things you do on the job—are more important than you could possibly imagine. And if you go into work every day with that attitude, you'll be so much closer to living a spiritual life.

The Family Who . . .

BY NOW, you've spent the better part of four weeks learning what makes you feel most spiritual. You've gone to church, listened to music, written in your journal, watched your golden retriever play. You meditate in the morning, read at night. You've stopped watching TV one day a week.

Chances are, your family has started to notice.

Maybe they're a little curious, too. *Why does Mom shut herself in her room for ten minutes? Why does Dad seem less stressed-out these days? Why is my sister saying blessings before meals? She always used to just dig in with the rest of us.*

If so, that's great. This week is the time to expand your spirituality to all corners of your life, and there's no better place to begin than with the people you love most.

You've heard the phrase "family unit" used so many times that it's almost a laughable cliché. But that's exactly what a solid family is—a core unit, bonded by blood, love, honor and trust, whose decisions are made for the good of everyone involved, with respect for the feelings of each individual.

Experts say that children cooperate best when they're made to feel as though they're part of a team. They may not clean their rooms just because Mom tells them to, but they'll do it if they understand that everyone in the house has a job to do and that working together makes the family home a comfortable and pleasant place to be. Regular family meetings, in which everyone has a chance to air his or her feelings, problems and opinions without criticism, further establishes that sense of teamwork and camaraderie.

The strongest couples are the ones who look at their relationships as flexible, yet unbreakable bonds. Their sense of unity helps make their children feel secure and loyal, and it prevents in-laws and friends from trying to coerce one spouse into a decision that might not be right for the other.

So if teamwork builds strong families, how much stronger might a family be if everyone in it is getting in touch with his or her spiritual nature? I won't repeat the other cliché about families who pray together, but there's no question that the best way to build a spiritual foundation is by starting at home. Even if the family members choose different paths later on, the basics will still have been established. Or, as in my case, those who don't choose to follow the family's spiritual course may change their minds somewhere down the road.

So your next assignment is to get at least one family member thinking about ways to become more spiritual. This may be one of the more difficult exercises you'll do, but it may also be one of the most rewarding.

"Yeah, sure," you might say. "*My* family? Dream on."

Honest, it's not as impossible as it might seem. As you've already observed, there are many wonderful ways to awaken to spirituality with a minimum of effort. There should be at least one way to appeal to even the most resistant soul.

Children, in particular, are spiritual creatures to begin with. The world is still new to them, and they respond to it with awe. Most have very little trouble with the concept of a Higher Power or a force of nature that causes the sun to rise and plants to spring from seeds. They're bursting with creativity, needing little or no prompting to pick up a journal, a paintbrush or a drum to express their deepest feelings. Besides, as any parent knows, children learn from example. If they see their parents praying or talking about God, they may not always join in—but they'll remember.

The key to introducing spirituality to other people—friends as well as family—is not to overwhelm them with information, enthusiasm, threats, expectations or demands. Would you have picked up this book if the title had been *You WILL Be a Perfectly Spiritual Person Right Now or Else You'll Be a Worthless Human Being for the Rest of Your Life*? Of course not. Or think about the religious sects who warn unbelievers that they must change their entire way of thinking instantaneously and completely or risk horrible damnation. This approach may win over some people, but if it worked on everyone, then the world would all have converted long ago. Besides, your goal isn't to "change" anyone in your family but to introduce them to ideas that they might find helpful in enriching their lives.

So keep it casual. Telling your loved ones, "I'm a more spiritual person now, and I want to help you become just like me" won't get you very far. Start with something simple. If you give yourself a period of silence every day, you could encourage your kids to join in. "I'm taking a quiet time now. How about we all get comfortable and just enjoy being together without talking?" If fights or giggling begin—which will inevitably happen—calmly send the offenders out of the room and say, "Sorry, but this is quiet time. Only people who are ready to be quiet can join in." It shouldn't be long before you get more cooperative volunteers.

See if you can find ways to bring up the topic naturally. If you and your young child are picking flowers, you could say, "I like to think that a great Spirit makes the flowers grow and the rain fall. What do you think? What do you think God looks like?" For older children, you could explore deeper waters: why bad things happen in the world, what they perceive their souls to be, how they feel when they go to church, what they know about world religion, ethical issues.

Or you could talk with your spouse or partner about establishing a spiritual practice as a family habit. At a family meeting, you might say, "We've noticed that we've all been so busy on weekends that we hardly ever have time to be together or to enjoy some downtime. So we're going to try an experiment. Starting next week, we'll start observing one Sunday every month as our family Sabbath. We'll put off the chores, turn off the TV and spend a quiet day at home together. What do you think? What kinds of things would you like to do?"

If your family already enjoys spiritual activities—going to religious services, praying, singing or saying grace before meals—talk to one or all of them about trying one of the other exercises shown here. A young child might have fun gardening; a teenager could probably use a few gossip-free days; your spouse will certainly be open to spiritual lovemaking.

Once you've introduced the idea or exercise to one or all of your family, don't be hurt or disappointed if they don't take to it right away. Sometimes it takes a while to get enthusiastic about the idea of personal spirituality. And don't let it discourage you from going ahead with your own quest. We all have our individual paths to follow. Not everyone experiences spirituality in the same way. Who knows—after a while, you might hear someone in your family say, "I could really use a few minutes of quiet" or "That looks like an interesting book—could I borrow it when you're done?"

Giving of Yourself

Now that you know more about the importance of good deeds, it's time to go a step farther. It's wonderful to bestow little day-brighteners that don't require much of us, but being spiritual also means that sometimes we have to expend more of our time, energy and money in order to make a difference.

You don't need me to tell you that there are people all over the world who live in conditions that seem almost incompatible with life. You know that people go hungry and homeless every day, that wars and natural disasters wreak havoc on small towns and large cities alike. You've seen enough news reports about AIDS and cancer, babies abandoned by their young mothers, drug abusers struggling to get clean, adults whose illiteracy keeps them from holding down a decent job, women who live in fear of the next broken bone and bruised eye, children, no longer innocent, who pretend to sleep, knowing their molester will come for them anyway. And though the deluded "duck and cover" days are long over, you know that we are still far from the kind of global peace that would guarantee that no country would ever again attempt to use nuclear power to destroy another.

There is much in the world that is good. But as long as there is also so much that is wrong, we cannot call ourselves truly spiritual if we don't at least try to alleviate the suffering of others.

So one day this week, make the time to at least look into opportunities for volunteer work. If you can only spare half an hour every week or two, that's fine; if you can do more, so much the better. Or maybe you'd rather focus on onetime events, such as a walk for breast cancer or a fundraiser to pay the expenses of a child who needs a bone marrow transplant.

Think about causes that are closest to your heart. You can't change every social ill, but choosing one you truly believe in will make you more motivated to keep on. Then look in your local Yellow Pages, on the Internet or call the local chapter of the United Way or your social services department for information on groups in your area that could use your help.

Some ideas:

· Join a local chapter of Habitat for Humanity and help construct a new house for a low-income family. (You don't have to be an expert carpenter or electrician; they'll give you a job suited to your abilities.)

· Work in a soup kitchen once or twice a week.
· Many hospitals need volunteers to feed and cuddle babies born with HIV or addicted to drugs. See if yours is one of them.
· Join a crisis hot line and help callers cope with problems ranging from marital disputes to depression and suicidal thoughts.
· If you're physically able, get the training necessary to become a volunteer firefighter or ambulance technician.
· Work at an animal shelter and help dogs and cats find good homes. (Millions of pets are abandoned every year.)
· Deliver hot meals to elderly men and women or to homebound AIDS patients. It may be the only food they get that day.
·Give blood. It takes just a few minutes, and a pint can save as many as five lives.
· Spend a few nights a month in a shelter that assists battered women.
· Spend time at a nursing home in your area. Help with the activities or just take the time to talk to the residents who may not see visitors for weeks. (My father has spent the last several years doing just that and finds it enormously rewarding.)
· Parents of disabled or autistic children often find their time, energy and emotions stretched to their limit. If you know of such a family, offer to babysit some afternoons or evenings.
· Be sure your children take UNICEF boxes when they go out on Halloween.

· Join an effort to clean up a trash-filled neighborhood or plant a community garden.
· Offer to entertain at a daycare center for children from low-income families.
· Tutor an illiterate adult or teach English to a recent immigrant.
· Ask about opportunities in cancer wards, houses of worship, psychiatric facilities, hospices, prisons, convents, farms or wherever your help is needed.

If it's absolutely impossible for you to give of your time now, then consider giving financially instead. Every contribution makes a difference. Some organizations allow you to have a set amount taken from your paycheck or bank account each month, so you don't have to think about writing out a check.

Showing concern for your fellow man may not guarantee you extra credit in God's ultimate report card. But the idea isn't to do good works simply to gain the favor of the universe or the Higher Power. Volunteer because it's part of a greater right. Do it because it may prove to be the turning point for another human being. Do it because there's no telling when you might need help one day. Give of yourself because in so doing, you enrich your soul and become more than what you are—and that's the goal of being spiritual in the first place.

Last Day: Looking Back

THE END OF THE MONTH already? It doesn't seem possible, does it? But yes, your thirty-day experiment in spirituality is at an end . . . at least this portion of it. As I've said before, discovering spirituality isn't something you start and finish in a month's time; it's a process that continues to grow and evolve as we do. This was just a taste of how much it can add to your life—and I hope it has made you hungry for more.

Now's the time to take account of what you've accomplished over the last few weeks. If you've been doing these exercises faithfully—or if you've tried only one— you've achieved a lot. You've taken that first step toward discovering who you and God are. And you've seen that it's not nearly as difficult or daunting as it may have appeared at first.

Sometime today, give yourself time to think about what you've learned. What did you enjoy most? What made you feel closest to God? Which exercises made you feel calmer or less stressed? Was there anything that *didn't* work, and if so, why?

If you started a spirituality journal, read your entries. Are there any patterns there? For example, do you seem most attuned to your soul when music is involved? Or nature or ritual or other people? What else could you be doing that involves those elements?

Take out the credo you wrote at the beginning of the month and read it again with a fresh eye. Does it still ring true to you, or has anything you've experienced in the last thirty days made you question or change a particular belief? Is there anything you want to add? Make additions or corrections as you see fit, then put your credo away again. See what happens if you return to it again next month or in six months or in a year's time. You might even want to keep a copy of your original paper in a safe place, perhaps as part of a time capsule or a personal history for your children or grandchildren to enjoy later.

Skim through this book again. Are there any exercises you didn't do that you'd like to try next month or sometime in the future? There's no need to rush to accomplish them all; this was just a kick-start. There's plenty of time to explore and discover new ways to seek God.

Perhaps you landed on one or two assignments that felt so good, you want to stick with them for a while. That's terrific. Keep practicing them until they become so ingrained within you that you can't imagine ever stopping.

Then, if you like, you can add more spiritual exercises to your daily routine.

Or maybe you're feeling guilty now because the month's already up and you don't have much to show for it. Maybe you didn't try as many of the assignments as you'd intended, or you tried one or two and couldn't get far. Don't beat yourself up about it. This isn't a test. Nobody's going to flunk you for not being "spiritual enough." But it might help to think about why this didn't work for you.

Was it hard to find the time to do the exercises you chose? If that's the case, then you might need to rearrange your personal priorities to make sure those ten or fifteen minutes are always there for you. We rarely avoid brushing our teeth or taking a bath because we run out of time. Think about it that way: You need to carve out that space to give your soul a refreshing, too.

Did you have trouble getting comfortable with the concept of communicating with God or with your soul? Then take it in smaller steps. Think about the times you feel a deep sense of awe and gratitude or an inner calm that defies explanation. Acknowledge those moments silently when they come—just be aware that they're there and how good they make you feel. Then try jotting down the incidents in a journal at least once a week. Or try meditating or a contemplative walk again. Once you become more familiar with the holy moments in your life, the idea of going through an exercise for a month may be more appealing to you.

Whatever you did this month, I hope you enjoyed it and that you've come away feeling better about yourself and your unique place in the greater scheme of things. I've learned a lot in both the writing of this book and in the events that led me to it, and I hope some of that knowledge came through in these pages.

I wish you much joy and many blessings.

I don't think I do things on a regular basis to make me feel spiritually fulfilled. If everyone from time to time, no matter what religion they are affiliated with—or if they are affiliated with none—would think about the axiom "Do unto others as you wish them to do unto you," or the negative side of it: "Do not do unto others what you wouldn't like them to do unto you," this thought would cause you to do something each day—big or small—that could lift your spirits.

In spite of all the killing that goes on around the world—and in spite of the fact that most of it is caused by differences in religion—all religions have something in common. The Muslims follow Muhammad, the Christians follow Jesus and the Jews follow Moses. We may take different routes, but we are all leading to the same destination: the God of Abraham. We forget how much we all have in common. If we think about it from time to time, that would make us better people, and that is what every religion strives to attain.

—KIRK DOUGLAS

Did any of the exercises in this book work for you? Do you have any spiritual practices of your own that you'd like to recommend to others? What are the most memorable spiritual moments you, or a friend or family member, have experienced? I'd love to hear your stories—and possibly include them in future books.

Send your anecdotes (original, please, and no more than four hundred words), along with your name, address and daytime phone number, to:

Aborn/Spiritual Life Stories
c/o Doubleday
1540 Broadway
New York, NY 10036